The Grandkid

The Grandkid

JOHN LAZARUS

Playwrights Canada Press
TORONTO

LIBRARY AND ARCHIVES CANADA CATALOGUING IN PUBLICATION
Lazarus, John, 1947-, author
    The grandkid / John Lazarus.

A play.
Issued in print and electronic formats.
ISBN 978-1-77091-213-7 (pbk.).-- ISBN 978-1-77091-214-4 (pdf).--
ISBN 978-1-77091-215-1 (epub)

    I. Title.

PS8573.A99G73 2014   C812'.54   C2013-908483-5
                                               C2013-908484-3

We acknowledge the financial support of the Canada Council for the Arts, the Ontario Arts Council (OAC)—an agency of the Government of Ontario, which last year funded 1,681 individual artists and 1,125 organizations in 216 communities across Ontario for a total of $52.8 million—the Ontario Media Development Corporation, and the Government of Canada through the Canada Book Fund for our publishing activities.

To Anne Levitsky,
my grade five teacher and lifelong friend,
for early and ongoing inspiration.

Playwright's Notes

Scene titles in the script are for rehearsal convenience, not for the audience's information.

All overlaps throughout the play, indicated with a forward slash (/), are optional and may begin later than indicated.

In the theatre cast list and bios, the characters are to be referred to as "Rothstein" and "Rothstein."

The Grandkid, produced by Theatre Kingston, received its premiere at the Baby Grand Theatre in Kingston, Ontario, on February 2, 2012, in a slightly different draft. It featured the following cast and creative team:

Rothstein: Sophia Fabiilli
Rothstein: Sam Malkin

Directed by Brett Christopher
Set design by Mark Hunt
Costumes by Cass Sclauzero
Lighting design by Tim Fort
Sound design by Becky Gold
Production management by Bill Penner
Technical direction by Alysha Bernstein
Stage management by, in succession, Kristi White, Brett Christopher, Amy Cadman, Alysha Bernstein, and Kyle Beres (it's a long story).

Characters

Julius Rothstein, sixty-seven and then sixty-eight. In the audience scenes he is a few years older; in the flashback scenes, he is in his fifties.

Abby Rothstein, his granddaughter, eighteen and then nineteen. In the audience scenes she is around thirty; in the flashback scenes, she is a little girl of five.

Setting

The living and dining room of Julius's home in a small university city in Ontario. The home is that of a film professor. It was decorated by his late wife, Phyllis, and reflects her tastes as much as his. The decor may also communicate that this is a Jewish home with both leftist and pro-Israeli political sympathies. Decoration includes a framed photo of Julius's deceased wife, Phyllis, a Jewish lady in her early sixties, and a large mirror on the wall, of antique, faded glass in an ornate frame. One door, from the dining room side, leads to the kitchen; another door leads off to the vestibule and front door; and a third door leads to the unseen rest of the house, which includes Abby's bedroom, Phyllis's sewing room, and the stairs to the second floor and Julius's bedroom. There are two other, smaller acting areas for the audience scenes.

Act One

AUDIENCE SCENE: ROTHSTEIN WAS OUR NAME

In the audience scenes, ABBY *and* JULIUS *address two different fictitious audiences, on two different occasions, and are unaware of each other.* ABBY, *thirtyish, wears a black scarf with a tear or cut in the fabric.* JULIUS, *in his seventies, wears a brightly coloured, hand-knit yarmulke and holds a champagne glass. They are these ages, with these accessories, in all of the audience scenes. In these scenes, their lines may overlap or be spoken simultaneously.*

ABBY First of all, I should give you fair warning: I am going to be referring to him as Rothstein, because that's what I always called him.

JULIUS For this joyful occasion, I will be referring to her as Abby—

ABBY Dad asked me not to, especially today.

JULIUS —Although ever since she was three or four, I've addressed her as Rothstein.

ABBY He asked me to call him Grandfather, Grandpa, Zaydie, or, as he put it, "something respectful like that."

JULIUS She addressed me as Rothstein too.

ABBY But it *was* respectful.

JULIUS Tells you something about our relationship.

ABBY He called me Rothstein right back. That was our name. *(continues simultaneously with JULIUS, below)* As Rothstein said, the only problem would be if we forgot which of us was which.

JULIUS *(simultaneously with ABBY, above)* I always used to say, the one pitfall might be forgetting which Rothstein was which.

ABBY'S ARRIVAL

Late night, early September. The house is a bit of a mess, with a couple of days' worth of untidiness created by someone not expecting guests. Books, clothes, newspapers. The doorbell rings. JULIUS, sixty-seven years old, in a bathrobe, crosses to the front door.

JULIUS *(calls through door)* Who the hell is it? It's after midnight!

ABBY *(off, eighteen years old)* Rothstein!

JULIUS   Yes, I'm Rothstein! Who are you!

ABBY   It's *me*, Rothstein! It's Rothstein!

JULIUS   Oh, for God's sake!

> *He opens the door to* ABBY, *dressed for travel, with luggage and a hockey stick in hand.*

Rothstein!

ABBY   Rothstein!

JULIUS   Ohmygod!

ABBY   Ohmygod!

JULIUS   You're, like, here!

ABBY   I am!

JULIUS   And so—soon!

ABBY   What?

JULIUS   No, wait, hug first. *(They hug.)* Rothstein! No way!

ABBY   Shut up!

JULIUS   Get out!

ABBY   Fuck off!

JULIUS   That's more like it. Wow. Look at you. I am so glad to see you. Place is a bit of a disaster, but, uh—

ABBY   You thought I was coming tomorrow.

JULIUS   Um, yes.

ABBY   It is tomorrow. Monday, twelve thirty A.M.

JULIUS   Oh, for God's sake, of course it is. I'm sorry. I been having a senior moment. For about a year now.

ABBY   Well, here I am.

    ABBY *starts moving her luggage inside.*

JULIUS   So you are! Let me help with— Oh my God, look at all this stuff. Jesus, don't / do all that yourself.

ABBY   No, it's okay, I got it.

JULIUS   *(helping her)* I thought young people were supposed to travel light.

ABBY   This is for the whole school year.

JULIUS   Course it is, don't mind me. God, you hear what I just said? "I thought young people..." I hate that kind of talk. I'm already stereotyping you. *(brief silence)* Hi.

ABBY   Hi.

JULIUS   I'm glad you're here.

ABBY   I know! Me too!

JULIUS   I know this is to save money, but I want it to be a good experience for both of us.

ABBY   Of course. I know it will. It's not just the money. It'll be lunky!

JULIUS   It will indeed be lunky.

ABBY   We'll get to know each other better.

JULIUS   Yeah. It'll be good to have some female energy in the house again.

ABBY   I guess you miss her a lot, eh?

JULIUS   Youthful female energy.

ABBY   Useful how?

JULIUS   No, *youth*ful.

ABBY   Oh. I thought you said "useful." Like, carrying stuff, mowing the lawn and shit.

JULIUS   Oh, well, maybe that too.

ABBY   Hey, that's part of the deal, we talked about this.

JULIUS   I know. We'll work out the details. I guess your friends think you're crazy, eh? Moving in with your old zaydie instead of in res.

ABBY   They just don't know my old zaydie.

JULIUS   That's right. That's right! *(regarding hockey stick)* You know, they do sell hockey sticks here in Ontario. We're very Canadian.

ABBY   This is my lucky stick. I've had it since I was fourteen. It's kind of my security blanket. I'm gonna try out for the women's team.

JULIUS   Great. I feel so stupid about getting the day wrong. Why didn't you phone me? You don't have to worry about waking me up, / I stay up late these days—

ABBY   I did. There wasn't any answer. Look, it's no big deal, I figured / you forgot and—

JULIUS   What? You phoned me? *(checks phone)* And I had the ringer off. I am so sorry.

ABBY   It's no biggie, really.

JULIUS   All right. You got here okay. Nu, you want something? Beer, wine, coffee, tea, water—

ABBY   I'll have a beer if you are. It'll be a trake.

JULIUS   Excellent, let's have a beer. *(as he exits to kitchen)* I don't remember "trake."

ABBY   It's a break with a treat in it. I emailed it to you. Couple years ago.

JULIUS   *(off)* Very nice. I don't remember all the gazorps [ga-ZORPS] you emailed. You used to come up with so many of them.

      Re-enters with the beers.

      Listen, I'm gonna pay you back for the cab. I was supposed to come pick you up at the train station.

ABBY   Bus station, / but anyway—

JULIUS   It starts our whole year off on a— Bus station? You took the bus?

ABBY   There's a bus that comes straight from Pearson.

JULIUS   So I would have gone to the wrong station anyway.

ABBY   Well, there you go.

JULIUS   So thank God I got the date wrong!

ABBY   Thank God!

JULIUS   L'chaim! *(They clink bottles.)*

ABBY   L'chaim! *(They drink.)*

JULIUS   Look at you. You look even better than ever.

ABBY   Thanks. You look—great.

JULIUS   When was the last time I saw you? In Victoria, February. Reading week. What's that, seven months?

ABBY   Almost.

JULIUS   You've changed. You look older, somehow. Which at your age is a good thing. A little more mature. Maybe I'm just seeing you differently, now you're a university student.

ABBY   I've aged. I am deeply aged.

JULIUS   You excited about starting classes?

ABBY   More like scared shitless. My friends at university say the classes are much harder.

JULIUS   Oh, you'll do great. You're a great student.

ABBY   Yeah, big fish in a small pond, in high school. Now it's the big pond. Full of sharks. How are you? Any movies?

JULIUS   Not at the moment. I've got another project happening. Trying to save the Loyalist.

ABBY   What? What's happening to the Loyalist?

JULIUS   It's falling apart. The Winterbottom family has to sell it. I want to get the university to buy it and keep it going as an art house. The nightmare is if some developer guts the thing and builds condos.

ABBY   That would be awful. I used to love that theatre.

JULIUS   Don't put it in the past tense quite yet. I'm gonna convince this colleague of mine, Rachel Zilber, to work with me. She and her husband Max are kind of a power couple in town. I want to put together a non-profit to restore the thing and sell it to the university.

ABBY   Cool. I can just hear Dad saying, "There he goes again, my hippie activist father."

JULIUS   And how is the Enemy in Common?

ABBY   He's fine. He knows we call him that, you know.

JULIUS   I know. It's an old Sam Levenson joke. My mother and David used to call *me* that. L'dor v'dor.

ABBY   Mom's fine too, by the way. They send their best. Although Dad thinks we won't last until Christmastime. He says we'll be at each other's throats by December.

JULIUS   Where does he get this shit?

ABBY   I know, eh?

JULIUS   This was his idea in the first place.

ABBY   I know!

JULIUS   How soon they forget! Oy, the stories I could tell you!

ABBY   Please don't. He just thinks we won't get along, 'cause he and I aren't getting along.

JULIUS   Why, what's wrong?

ABBY   Oh, nothing. Just stuff. Anyway, we'll show him, eh?

JULIUS   Oh hell yes, we'll show him. I am mean, I am clean, I am pumped, I am ready for you, kiddo. Whether it looks like it or not. I'm in better shape than I used to be. It's ironic. She dies of a heart attack, so I start exercising.

ABBY   Better late than never.

JULIUS   Too late for her.

ABBY   Yeah, but not for you.

JULIUS   Yeah. Notice anything else about the house? I mean besides the mess, which is temporary.

ABBY   Uh, not really.

JULIUS   The smell. The cigarette smell.

ABBY   Yeah?

JULIUS   Gone! Right?

ABBY   No.

JULIUS   No? Oh. Well, I quit in March.

ABBY   You did! Sweet! Mazel tov!

JULIUS   Thanks. I'm embarrassed about how it all looks, though. I'm not really this much of a slob. I was gonna clean up tomorrow.

ABBY   Can I see my room?

JULIUS   Yeah, but your room's the worst. I been using it to store stuff. Cartons and plastic bins that I haven't put in the basement. And the bed's not made. Nothing's ready.

ABBY   You got clean sheets?

JULIUS   Yes! I am at least the proud owner of clean sheets.

ABBY   So I'll make the bed and we'll clean up together tomorrow.

> *She starts to exit, stops, and looks at the antique mirror.*

That mirror used to scare me when I was little. The distortions.

JULIUS   Yeah, the glass is warped, it's really old. That mirror came over with Phyllis's grandmother.

ABBY   Yeah? I like it now.

> *She exits. A brief silence.*

(off) Yeah, it's a storage tank, all right. What are you doing with Bubbie Phyllis's sewing room?

JULIUS   Take a look.

> *A silence, then* ABBY *re-enters.*

ABBY   It's like she just stepped out for a second.

JULIUS   You think?

ABBY   It's strange seeing all her work files still there. And that dress that's still in the sewing machine. I remember her in that dress. When I was little.

JULIUS   Yeah. She still liked it. She was putting sleeves on it.

ABBY   It's almost like it's, uh—

Beat.

JULIUS   What?

ABBY   Like it's waiting for her.

JULIUS   Yes.

A brief silence.

ABBY   I thought you might have got rid of the machine. But I figured, if it was still in the house, like, in the basement or something, I was going to ask if I could use it. 'Cause, you know, a lot of the clothes I wore, growing up, she made for me on that machine. And that's where she taught me to sew. We had a lot of good talks over that machine. But I didn't expect it to still be in the room like that. With her dress still in it. So, you know, if you don't want me to use it, I understand perfectly. I just can't tell if the room's like that because you just haven't bothered to do anything with it, or because you're—um—preserving it.

JULIUS   Me neither.

A brief silence.

ABBY   Well, you don't have to decide now.

JULIUS   No.

ABBY   I could finish the dress. If you want.

JULIUS   Oh, boy. Oy.

ABBY   I didn't mean to—

JULIUS   I just have to think about that.

ABBY   Okay.

JULIUS   Just let me think about it.

ABBY   Sure.

HOUSE RULES

The next morning. The remains of breakfast are on the dining table. During this scene ABBY busies herself cleaning up while JULIUS takes it easy.

JULIUS   So! First day!

ABBY   Stop saying that. I'm scared enough as it is.

JULIUS   You know your way around campus?

ABBY   Just your office and the cafeteria next door. Otherwise, wilderness.

JULIUS   So after breakfast I'll show you around.

ABBY   Okay. I have to be at a frosh meet-and-greet at one thirty.

JULIUS   That works. We'll have time. But I thought we'd start by establishing some rules.

ABBY   Rules?

JULIUS   Not mom-and-dad type rules. More, you know, equal partners in a household. Like in a dorm! If you were living in a dorm you'd all be getting together to make rules. Wouldn't you?

ABBY   I have no idea.

JULIUS   Sure you would. So just think of me as your dormmate.

ABBY   Yeah, I'll work on that.

JULIUS gives her a sheet of paper.

JULIUS   Here's a schedule of the garbage and recycling. We can alternate, week by week.

ABBY   You know what, maybe we should just be cleaning up this morning, just get it done, instead of working on rules for the future.

JULIUS   Yeah, yeah, we'll clean up, but this could be fun! Gimme a rule!

ABBY   You first.

JULIUS   Okay. No parties without the other one's consent.

ABBY   Okay.

JULIUS   Okay? Wow, that was easy. Okay. Now you.

ABBY   Um—what happens at Rothstein's stays at Rothstein's. No cute stories in class about shit your granddaughter says.

JULIUS   Or your grandfather. Agreed. It's about equal respect, right? Two grown-ups sharing a home. Not, you know, Gidget and Grandpa.

ABBY   Who's Gidget?

JULIUS   Oh, I have one. I want you to phone first if you're bringing a guy home for the night.

ABBY   Eeewww.

JULIUS   Now if you don't mind my meeting them—

ABBY   "*Them*"? Whaddaya mean, "them"!

JULIUS   I mean one at a time.

ABBY   There's not gonna be any "them," one at a time or in a pile! Jesus.

JULIUS   Don't get indignant. You're an adult. Wouldn't you rather we covered this in advance? Or are you offended 'cause I'm implying you're gonna be unfaithful to Warren?

ABBY   No. Warren and I broke up.

JULIUS   Ah. Why? Oh, sorry, never mind.

ABBY   No, it's okay. It was just time. And Dad was kind of a factor.

JULIUS   Oh, yeah? How?

ABBY   Don't say it like that! You don't have to light up every time I criticize him!

JULIUS   I know I don't have to. David was a factor how?

ABBY   He found out we were having sex.

JULIUS   He didn't know?

ABBY   Go figure. We never kept it a secret. But I think he thought I was a virgin.

JULIUS   Really?

ABBY   Yeah, I know, eh? Anyway, he started treating us like twelve-year-olds without a clue. Lecturing us on birth control. We're eighteen, and we were being responsible. But he got so freaked out!

JULIUS   Does he still want you to be a lawyer?

ABBY   You have to be a virgin to be a lawyer?

JULIUS   No, honey, I'm changing the subject.

ABBY   Yeah, he does. He was so glad to hear I'm taking soshe. I made a point of telling him it's a prereq for law school.

JULIUS   And where does Vanessa stand?

ABBY   She's decided I'm gonna be a teacher like her.

JULIUS   Where do they get this stuff? I never told David what to do with his life. It's your life! Don't let them tell you what to be!

ABBY   I know. I won't.

JULIUS   Right! Because you're a filmmaker! Always have been! So you've enrolled in Film 100?

ABBY   Uh, no.

JULIUS   No? Well, get on it! You have to start with that, it's the prereq for all the other film courses, and I'm teaching it.

ABBY   Uh—Rothstein—I'm not taking film.

JULIUS   You're not?

ABBY   No.

JULIUS   I just assumed you'd—you've had cameras ever since you were little.

ABBY   Yeah, and they were fun, but for my career I want to do something—

         Beat.

JULIUS   Serious?

ABBY   I wasn't going to say that. Sociological, I guess. Hands
            on. Don't know what yet, but / it'll have something—

JULIUS   Not knowing yet is a very creative place to be, in your
            situation.

ABBY   Oh, well, good, 'cause I so totally don't. I sort of picture
            myself in a Third World country. Helping people, some-
            how. Correcting injustice. Hands on. I know, it probably
            sounds like the spoiled naive First World kid who thinks
            she can go / save everybody—

JULIUS   No, not at all! I mean, not much.

ABBY   It's just that Dad is a white Jewish Canadian and Mom
            is a white Protestant Canadian and they both act like it's
            this amazingly courageous mixed-race family. I want to
            raise the bar. Work somewhere really different. And have
            an effect, you know?

JULIUS   You could always *minor* in film.

ABBY   Sorry. I've already chosen my courses.

JULIUS   I don't get to teach you? I guess I had this fantasy of
            having you in class and treating you just like every-
            body else.

ABBY   Okay, look, you want a rule? How's this for a rule? No
            telling Abby what to do with her life. Can that be a rule?

JULIUS   Oy. Yeah. That can be a rule.

SHABBOS

Morning. JULIUS *enters in shirt sleeves and a plain yar-mulke, and knocks on* ABBY's *door.*

JULIUS   Hey, sleepy, let's go. It's eight thirty.

ABBY   *(off)* What?

JULIUS   Lemme know if you want the shower. Also, I'm making breakfast.

ABBY   *(off)* It's Saturday.

JULIUS   My point exactly. Good Shabbos.

Somewhere here she enters in a housecoat.

The service starts at ten. And by the way, honey, thanks for doing the laundry yesterday, but you only did the dark stuff. I have a white shirt I like to wear to shul, but today I have to wear a different one. It's a small thing, I know, but anyway.

He begins to exit to the kitchen.

ABBY   Okay, sorry. Rothstein?

JULIUS   Yeah?

ABBY   Uh, well, I'm not going.

JULIUS   *(pause)* Today, or generally?

ABBY   Both. Neither.

JULIUS   *(pause)* When did this happen?

ABBY   A while back.

JULIUS   *(pause)* Okay. So go back to sleep. Or lemme know if you want breakfast.

> *He begins to exit again.*

ABBY   Zaydie.

> *JULIUS stops.*

You okay with this?

JULIUS   Look, it's your business. I just assumed you'd be going. We always went to shul when we got together, right? So, you know, I'm surprised. Did you change your mind over the summer?

ABBY   No, I changed my mind before my bat mitzvah.

JULIUS   Before your—when you were *twelve*?

ABBY   Dad said he just wanted me to get through the bat mitz-vah, and after that it was my decision. So I stopped going. So then he stopped going.

JULIUS   Ah. Vanessa, right?

ABBY   What do you mean?

JULIUS   Well, you know.

ABBY   What? Dad married a shiksa who won't let him go
         to shul?

JULIUS   No, but she could influence him in some way.

ABBY   She had no objection to our going to shul. She never
         tried to discourage us. In fact, she got Dad to switch to
         Reform so I could *have* a bat mitzvah, 'cause our old shul
         wouldn't let me 'cause she's not Jewish.

JULIUS   Yeah, I knew that, and that was very nice. But just being
         there, being his wife, your mom, a Christian...

ABBY   She's not a Christian. Not really. She's not anything.

JULIUS   Are *you* anything?

ABBY   I guess not. It's not something I think about much. I kind
         of like Buddhism from a distance.

JULIUS   No offence, but I don't understand people who don't
         believe in God. I don't know what they use to get through.

ABBY   No offence, but I don't know how intelligent adults can
         believe those old folk tales.

JULIUS   You don't believe with your intelligence. It goes deeper.
         You just feel a presence, sometimes. Not in shul, strangely
         enough. Shul is more about community, about getting in

touch with the tribe. But if I didn't go to shul, I wouldn't have those other moments.

A brief pause.

Are you at least coming to Bubbie Phyllis's unveiling?

ABBY   Well, of course I am!

JULIUS   Good. Okay. It's next month. October twentieth.

ABBY   Okay.

JULIUS   So you're saying, when the four of us went to shul, this was fake? You sat there and spoke the words of prayers you didn't believe in?

ABBY   I think a lot of people do that.

JULIUS   I know. That's their problem.

ABBY   I kept trying to talk Dad out of going, but he insisted, he said it was for you. Maybe you should take it up with him.

JULIUS   I will. Next time. Absolutely.

ABBY   Uh huh. Add it to your list of stuff to talk to Dad about.

JULIUS   What?

ABBY   Well, you guys are pretty good at not talking to each other about shit.

JULIUS   Excuse me, but you've already made me upset enough for one Shabbos. You don't need to start in on my relationship with my son.

ABBY   Sorry.

JULIUS   I'll call him. I'll call him soon.

ABBY   Sure.

JULIUS   I promise.

ABBY   Whatever.

JULIUS   Absolutely.

ABBY   Okay.

JULIUS   Okay. So in the meantime, I'm making breakfast. You want a couple of eggs?

ABBY   Please.

JULIUS   Sorry we're fresh out of bacon.

    JULIUS exits.

AUDIENCE SCENE: GAZORPIMOSITY

ABBY   When I was five, he and I were walking his dog Herschel together, and I asked him where words come from. And he said—

JULIUS *(in his fifties, wearing the woollen cap referred to later)* People make them up. Except maybe for some words that God made up for us. You want to hear the oldest word in the world?

ABBY   *(age five)* Sure.

JULIUS The oldest word is "B'reysheet." That's Hebrew for "in the beginning." It's the first word in the Bible. Even before the name of God. So it's the oldest.

ABBY   What's the newest word?

JULIUS "Gazorpimosity." [ga-ZORP-i-MOS-i-ty] Gazorpimosity is the mixed feeling of annoyance and affection that you get when you're watching your dog pee on your neighbour's garbage can.

ABBY   *(to dog)* Herschel! *(to JULIUS)* You just made that word up!

JULIUS Course I did. How d'you think it got to be the newest word in the world?

ABBY   *(in her thirties, to audience)* So this was magic. Out of all the billions of people in the world, we had the newest word. But as Rothstein said—

JULIUS   Course, somebody else could invent a newer one at any moment.

ABBY   Saying that was his big mistake. Because from then on I insisted we keep inventing new words. We called them "gazorps." One day he'd promised to take me to the water park, but then he thought he had to cancel, but then it turned out we could go after all. And on the way home I said that thinking we wouldn't be able to go made it even more fun, because afterwards we felt lucky. And then I announced a gazorp for an extra special kind of fun you have when you're lucky. I said, you put the words "fun" and "luck" together, and I announced the word.

JULIUS   Kiddo—that's one of those words you don't say until you're a grown-up, and even then you have to be careful. You ever hear of the F-word? That's the F-word.

ABBY   *(age five)* No it's not. The F-word is "fart," everybody knows that.

JULIUS   Uh, no, honey. "Fart" is kind of borderline, but that word is the official F-word. Please don't say it. People will think you're a rude little girl, and your parents will think I'm teaching you bad words. Okay?

ABBY   Okay.

   Pause.

   Rothstein?

JULIUS   Oy...

ABBY   What does it mean?

JULIUS   Uh, well, strangely enough, it actually means an extra special kind of fun you have when you're lucky.

JULIUS'S SCRAPBOOK

Daytime, late September. ABBY *enters through the front door, in bicycling clothes for a day in autumn. She wears a helmet.*

ABBY   Well, that was pretty lunky. The fall colours here are amazing. Victoria ain't got nothin' like—Rothstein? Hello?

She calls back through the door.

Are you okay?

JULIUS   *(off, out of breath)* Of course I'm okay— Why wouldn't I be—okay?

ABBY   What's keeping you?

JULIUS   *(off)* I'm having a little trouble—with the bike lock— Okay. There we go.

ABBY   *(has removed her helmet)* I do like Bubbie Phyllis's helmet.

JULIUS   *(enters, also in biking clothes)* Glad you like it. You have some of her—raffish charm—in it. Water.

ABBY   *(gives him a bottle of water)* I got video of you on the bike.

JULIUS   Oh, really?— See?— You still—shoot video. *(drinks)*

ABBY   I got news for you. Everybody shoots video.

         She takes a cellphone out of her pocket.

JULIUS   Yeah— I'm well aware—thanks—but you—*always* shot video. Anyway—no putting that on YouTube until I get a look at it first.

ABBY   Okay.

JULIUS   You are in great shape, kiddo— I'm impressed— You're a real athlete. Now I see why you got on the hockey team.

ABBY   Thanks. Hey, we had our first meeting yesterday. I'm gonna be right wing.

JULIUS   Right wing?

ABBY   On the ice.

JULIUS   Oh. Well, that's great!

ABBY   *(offering cellphone)* Want to see yourself on the bike?

JULIUS   No, I can't face it. Pathetic, doddering old fart, wobbling all over the road.

ABBY   *(looking at video)* You are not. You're in better shape than you were. Like you said.

JULIUS   Thanks.

ABBY   On the other hand, I gotta say, the Loyalist has sure seen better days.

JULIUS   Oh, it's falling apart, nobody disputes that. The screen's gone to ratshit, the projector's flerged—what's really tragic is, it never had a proper final screening. I was there the night it closed. The projector broke down during the movie and they gave us all our money back, and the next day they announced that was it.

ABBY   First theatre I ever saw a movie in. You took me.

JULIUS   I know, I remember. It feels like six months ago.

ABBY   I was five.

JULIUS   Like I say: six months ago.

ABBY   I guess the place means a lot to you, eh?

JULIUS   It's not just sentiment. The whole concept of the movie palace was Canadian. When the Americans were showing movies in barns and warehouses, we were building theatres like the Loyalist: ornate interiors, plush seats. Then when Hollywood hijacked the Canadian industry, they stole the concept, too. But the Winterbottom family have hung on to this one, bless their flinty old Ontario hearts and their flinty old money. You want to join the fight to save it? We'll want some students on the committee.

ABBY   It's not really my style.

JULIUS   "Style"? What about the fun of it? These things are fun!

ABBY   I know. Knock yourself out. I look forward to hearing all about it.

JULIUS   I thought you were such an activist. Your gay-straight alliance in high school.

ABBY   Yeah, but this is just going to be a bunch of old, white, rich professors, isn't it? Saving a nice old building?

JULIUS   It's not just a nice old building, and we're not just—I'm not— Okay, that's it.

       He gets a photo album down from a shelf.

       Time to educate you about your heritage. Here. Check it out.

       He opens the album to a specific page and shows her a photo.

ABBY   Ohmygod, is that *you*? What's going on here? You're getting arrested! You're bleeding!

JULIUS   Yeah. Your grandfather has a criminal record. Didn't know that, did you? This was at a legalize-pot rally in Montreal.

ABBY   Look at you, flashing the peace sign at the camera. You were such a rebel!

JULIUS   This is where you get your activist gene.

ABBY   From you smoking weed?

JULIUS   It wasn't about smoking, it was about not getting locked *up* for smoking. It's still a valid cause. Sure, things are changing, but people still get busted.

ABBY   Your hair is un-frickin-believable.

JULIUS   You know what's really sad? That hirsute young man is the guy I still expect to see in the mirror.

ABBY   This is so cool. *(turns pages)* Okay, so this is you—Bubbie Phyllis—and this is Hannah?

JULIUS   That is my darling Hannah. That's the only picture I have of me and both my wives. This is at McGill. I was dating Hannah, and Phyllis was Hannah's best friend. Then Phyllis was the maid of honour at our wedding. Then, in 1969, Hannah died, in the famous car crash—

ABBY   How old were you guys?

JULIUS   Twenty-five. Both of us.

ABBY   God, that's young. That is, like, harsh.

JULIUS   Yeah, well, whatever. Anyway, it inspired me to make my great cinematic masterpiece, *Low Visibility*. Phyllis showed up at the first screening, which was here, at the Loyalist, and it was kind of an emotional moment, and we got together that night. We told each other Hannah would approve. And a year later we got married, and David got born.

ABBY   That's a story. That would make a movie.

JULIUS   It's interesting: some of the pivotal moments in my life have been at the Loyalist.

ABBY   What's your friend saying about it? The Loyalist?

JULIUS   Rachel? She is not encouraging. She doesn't think it can survive as a theatre, competing with the big chains. It doesn't have their stereo subwoofers and 3-D capability and shit. She says the university won't buy a theatre nobody's gonna come to.

ABBY   It's too bad Canadian movies suck.

JULIUS   What's that supposed to mean?

ABBY   Oh, not yours, of course. I'm just saying you could turn it into a pretty cool museum of Canadian film, if there was any history to put in it.

JULIUS   Oh my God, Rothstein. In your typical Canadian ignorance of your own cultural history you have stumbled on a brilliant idea.

ABBY   Don't patronize me, Rothstein.

JULIUS   There's plenty of history to put in it! We could keep the main auditorium for screenings, and there's a lot of smaller rooms in that building. There's a great film centre in Toronto, but this could be more like a *museum*, with the added charm of being out here in the boonies. This is brilliant! I'm phoning Rachel in the morning.

ABBY   Sweet. Just name a room after me.

JULIUS   Absolutely. The Abby Rothstein Hockey Movie Collection.

ABBY   Excellent. *(turns a page)* What's this? You, Phyllis, and—that little brat is Dad?

JULIUS   Yeah. With the car, en route to Toronto, like a Canadian *Grapes of Wrath.* I got sporadic work with the Film Board, and Phyllis, thank God, got her first full-time job in human resources at the hospital, which is what kept us going for a long time. This was in seventy-six, when the Parti Québécois got into power and a lot of Jews left Montreal. Even when they took power, the francophones kept acting like an oppressed minority, so they started to turn into an oppressor without realizing it. Ironic.

ABBY   Like Israel.

JULIUS   Excuse me?

ABBY   Well, the Jews were, like, oppressed for centuries, right? And then they got their own country, and they still feel threatened, so they turn around and do it to the Palestinians.

JULIUS   They don't "feel" threatened. Israel is surrounded by hostile nations who want to drive the Jews into the sea.

ABBY   Yeah, but they have the backing of all the—maybe we shouldn't talk about this.

JULIUS   The Québécois suffered nothing like how the Jews suffered! In 1774, under the Quebec Act, the anglos let them keep their own religion, language, and law! There's no comparison with how the Jews have been oppressed!

ABBY   Okay.

JULIUS   Uh huh. Well, here's something we didn't know about each other, eh. I didn't know you were anti-Israeli.

ABBY   I'm not, I'm just—

JULIUS   Pro-Palestinian? The Palestinians aren't even a real people! They're a fictional construct!

ABBY   I'm not pro or anti anybody. I don't know enough about this stuff to argue with you.

JULIUS   Clearly.

ABBY   Oh, man. You do have that profester streak in you, don't you.

JULIUS   "Profester" streak? Is that an old gazorp?

ABBY   No. I just made it up for the occasion.

PHONE YOUR PARENTS

Evening. JULIUS *and* ABBY *are both reading.*

JULIUS *(without looking up)* When are you gonna phone your parents?

> ABBY *looks up at him. He continues reading. Then he looks up and sees her looking at him. Pause.*

I ask merely out of curiosity. Housemately curiosity.

ABBY I've already phoned them twice since I got here. And they've phoned me. Plus texts.

JULIUS Oh, really? I didn't know that.

ABBY Why don't *you* ever phone them? You said you would phone Dad.

JULIUS I phone David.

ABBY You phone him on his birthday, he phones you on your birthday.

> *Pause.*

JULIUS We don't have a lot to talk about. We love each other, but we actually don't have that much in common. I don't know much about his work and he doesn't know much about mine.

ABBY   It has to be about work?

JULIUS   No, usually we talk about you. But otherwise we don't always know what to say. There's awkward silences. Anyway, I'm not his nineteen-year-old daughter starting college.

ABBY   I'll be phoning them once a week.

JULIUS   Oh? This is a deal you made with them?

ABBY   No, it's a deal I'm making with you, so you'll get off my ass about it.

JULIUS   Deal.

They resume reading.

BIRTHDAY PARTY

Evening, late September. JULIUS *and* ABBY *are eating a small birthday cake. Some gift wrap lies on the table.* JULIUS *wears* ABBY's *gift to him: a brightly coloured hand-knit toque that matches the yarmulke he wears in his audience scenes. Both have been drinking wine.*

ABBY   And it would be such a cool course! If anybody besides this Professor Greenleaf was teaching it. You know this guy?

JULIUS   Yeah. Major scholar. A bit full of himself, but he's got a lot of self to be full of.

ABBY   Yeah, no shit. We have to write this big paper, starting next term. He's easing us in 'cause we're just frosh.
But I'm way ahead. I know what I want to write about.
There's these ancient Aboriginal sisters in a village in
Brazil. They're the only two people left who speak the
Saliguando language. So everybody's descended on
these two old ladies to record their language. But they
won't play along. One of them stole the other one's husband forty years ago, and they haven't spoken to each
other since, even though the husband's been dead for
like decades. So these ladies are saying their language is
obsolete, 'cause neither of them uses it anymore, so there's
nothing to record. Some people say they have no right to
let a whole language go down the tubes just 'cause they're
pissed off at each other. My paper's gonna say they have
the right. It's their language. They own it.

JULIUS   Interesting.

ABBY   Yeah, eh? I got this idea, that two people can own a language, from our gazorps.

JULIUS   Of course.

ABBY   So do we have a duty to share the gazorps with everybody else?

JULIUS   No, but you and I invented gazorps. These ladies inher-
ited their language. Public domain.

ABBY   Hey, if they inherit it, they own it. I think. Anyway, I'm
having a lot of fun arguing it.

JULIUS   Excellent. You stick to your guns, then. Also, excellent cake, Rothstein.

ABBY   Thank you, Rothstein. You can thank my shiksa mother, who taught me to bake.

JULIUS   Noted. My thanks to your shiksa mother. Also for teaching you to knit. I love the toque and matching yarmulke concept.

He removes the toque, revealing the yarmulke from the audience scenes.

It's like a Canadian Jewish identity kit.

ABBY   That was the idea. How's sixty-eight so far?

JULIUS   It's just a strangely high number. It doesn't sound like me. I always wonder if every generation was this surprised to get old, or just us boomers.

ABBY   When I turn sixty-eight I'll let you know.

JULIUS   Thanks, I look forward to that.

The phone rings. He picks it up, looks at the caller ID, and speaks into the phone.

Hello, Rachel!... Oh, thank you! That is so thoughtful!... Yeah, Virgo... Uh, well, supposedly, a perfectionist and a neatnik.

ABBY   Hah.

JULIUS   Oh, just very quiet. My granddaughter Abby made me a beautiful birthday dinner... No, sixty-*eight*... Yeah, soixante-neuf is next year.

ABBY   Rothstein!

JULIUS   Actually, the last soixante-neuf was about twenty years ago.

ABBY   Don't be gross.

JULIUS   Yeah, that's Abby keeping me in line. I told you, eh, the film museum was her idea?... Have you mentioned it to Max?... Yeah, good, I thought he would... Oh, okay! *(to ABBY)* Party at Max and Rachel's house, next Saturday. *(as he writes on a calendar)* I'm pencilling you in... Yeah, my God, it's gonna be October already. What?... Well, I'll be there for sure, but I can't speak for Abby.

    ABBY *is shaking her head emphatically.*

    Uh, just a second, ask her yourself. *(to ABBY)* It's for you. Say hi to Professor Zilber.

    He gives ABBY *the phone.*

ABBY   Hello?... Yes, hi, Professor Zilber... It's going okay... Well, there's a lot of pressure this time of year... Oh, thank you, I just kind of said the museum thing as a joke and Roths—my grandfather got all excited about it... Okay! Sure, I'd love to come, thanks... Okay, yeah, I look forward to meeting you too... Okay, bye.

JULIUS   You sounded so shy!

ABBY   I get self-conscious talking to real Jews. Besides you. I'm always afraid they'll find out I don't know the secret handshake.

JULIUS There was no handshake, she was on the phone.

ABBY   Is this party gonna be all professors?

JULIUS No, Max and Rachel's parties, there's usually some students. Grad students, mostly.

ABBY   Do I have to actually go?

JULIUS You just said you were going!

ABBY   'Cause you put me on the spot! I'll have the flu or something.

JULIUS Aw, come on, it'll be fun, there'll be guests your age. This is important to me. For the museum. She's already talking about forming a committee. I don't want this to get away from me. I need to get in tight with these people.

ABBY   By showing them what a good grandpa you are? With me as arm candy?

JULIUS You are not "arm candy." At least nobody thinks—uh, nothing.

ABBY   What?

JULIUS Well, sometimes I worry that people see us together and think you're not actually my grandkid. That we're actually—you know.

ABBY   *Oh*! Oh, God, no, *nobody* thinks *that*.

JULIUS   They don't?

ABBY   Oh, God, no. I mean, look at me, and look at you!
          Nobody thinks that.

JULIUS   *(disappointed)* Oh. Good.

ABBY   Oh, don't worry, *nooobody* / thinks that.

JULIUS   Okay, I got it, thanks.

ABBY   Anyway, you're better off going to this thing without me.

JULIUS   All right, I can't force you to come.

ABBY   Good. 'Cause this is so blorched on so many levels. It's
          my idea, which you told her about, so why is it her com-
          mittee? And why do you have to impress her to get on
          it? And why do you have to use me to impress her? And
          why are you obsessing on this museum in the first place?

JULIUS   I want to keep on making a contribution. Besides the
          teaching. I run into old friends in Toronto, I want to be
          able to / tell them—

ABBY   But you're not some museum guy! You're a filmmaker!
          And what's wrong with teaching, as a contribution?
          All your students are making videos, they're all over
          YouTube.

JULIUS   I know. I don't watch them.

ABBY   How can you not watch them? They're your students!

JULIUS   That's why! I spend most of my working hours watch-
           ing student videos. And, frankly, this job is wearing me
           down. I'm getting deeply tired of student videos. With
           all due respect.

ABBY   Are you jealous of them?

JULIUS   Kids making videos? Good God, why?

ABBY   'Cause back in your day it was so hard and expensive to
           get the equipment and stuff. Now, anybody can do it.

JULIUS   Okay, first of all, please don't say "back in your day." My
           day is today. Not just 'cause it's my birthday. My day is
           always today.

ABBY   How Zen.

JULIUS   Second, it's great that anybody can make a video, but the
           downside is, anybody can make a video. Warhol didn't
           go far enough. We've got to the point where every minute
           in the world is famous for fifteen people.

ABBY   Are you ever gonna make another movie? 'Cause I always
           thought you would.

JULIUS   You have to choose today to do this?

ABBY   You just said, every day is today.

JULIUS   Cute. No, I am probably never gonna make another
           movie.

ABBY   Look, I found a screenplay in my room—

JULIUS   Oh, this house is full of student screenplays.

ABBY   No, yours. *Scarborough Bluffs*.

JULIUS   Oh, my God. Nineteen-twenty-three, it was, I remember it well.

ABBY   Nineteen-eighty-two, it was. You wrote it right after *Low Visibility*. I hope you don't mind; I started reading it.

JULIUS   Oh, please. It's cringe-making. There's no stakes. He quits painting so he can make money teaching, and then quits teaching to / go back to—

ABBY   Don't spoil it!

JULIUS   To go back to his art, which is more balls than *I* ever had, and anyway, why couldn't he do both, and anyway, who gives a fuck? I can't believe I still have a copy of that.

ABBY   It's good. It does so have stakes. You could do it mumblecore! Do it cheap! It's like you said, anybody / can do it—

JULIUS   *This is my birthday*! I *don't need* this on my *birthday*!

ABBY   Jesus, chill.

JULIUS   I do this enough to myself! Look, one thing *Scarborough Bluffs* will teach you: I've had an easy life. I been a straight white male in Canada. I grew up in a comfy middle-class home, never starved, I was never abused, bashed, or victimized, as a Jew or anything else. Just between us, I look at Canadian movies by, you know, gay people who grew up Catholic, or refugees with Muslim names—movies about death and oppression and cities on fire—and I think, "Well, sure, some people have all the luck."

ABBY   You've had pain. Both your wives died.

JULIUS   Yeah, well, the first one, I made that movie, so the second one I'm not gonna make it again.

     Pause.

     Okay, also, I don't like how the industry has evolved in this country, Rothstein. I don't like the part it steals from Hollywood, and I don't like the part that's uniquely, idiotically Canadian. First we had a slow start anyway, thanks to their studios coming up and acting like organized crime to shut us down and take over. Then our own government obligingly took over the job of choking off our own industry, under Hollywood's instructions. Then, just after *Low Visibility*, they came up with their famous hundred-percent tax shelter, so any plastic surgeon with too much money could call himself a film producer. It was a joke. So I got this here job and started making a living. Only, unlike the guy in *Scarborough Bluffs*, I haven't gone back. 'Cause I don't like where it's got to now either, all this Hollywood bullshit, with the pitching and the catching and developing the concept and comparing their dicks. So, for those and other reasons, here I sit, dug in at the diploma factory, fit for nothing but teaching.

ABBY   I thought you liked teaching.

JULIUS I have loved teaching. Until recently. I've been very lucky in my life. But like I say, that's kind of been the problem. Sorry. Sorry, honey, but I'm going to bed. Thank you. Thanks to you and your shiksa mother for the dinner and the cake and the Jewish Canadian ID kit.

He kisses her.

Sorry.

And exits.

AUDIENCE SCENE: ROTHSTEIN THE SNOWMAN

ABBY The thing about calling each other Rothstein started with a lullaby. When I was about three or four, I got "Frosty the Snowman" wrong. I called it "Rothstein the Snowman." And oh my God, the hilarity this caused in the family.

JULIUS When she was a little girl, Phyllis and I were visiting them in Victoria.

ABBY So Rothstein and Bubbie Phyllis were visiting from Ontario, and one night he was putting me to bed.

JULIUS And I had the honour of tucking her in for the night.

ABBY And I asked him to sing "Rothstein the Snowman."

JULIUS And she requested a song called "Rothstein the Snowman," so I did my best to come up with some lyrics.

ABBY   He didn't even pause for breath.

JULIUS   *(singing, as a lullaby)* Rothstein the snowman
         Was a jolly, happy soul,
         With an old hash pipe and a Jewish nose,
         And a brother-in-law named Joel.

JULIUS
& ABBY   *(sing)* Rothstein the snowman
         Is meshugeneh, they say,
         He's so full of crap, with his woollen cap,
         And his hair all turning grey.

         There must have been some smoked meat in
         That sandwich that they found,
         'Cause when they stuck it in his mouth,
         He did not make a sound.

             JULIUS exits.

ABBY   *(continues)* Oh, Rothstein the snowman
         Was as nuts as he could be,
         And the kids would say, "Won't you go away,
         'Cause you're really bugging me."

ABBY'S LAUNDRY STORY

Late evening, October. Enter JULIUS *from the party.*

JULIUS   *(removing coat)* Unbelievable. They actually went ahead and bought it.

        ABBY *enters after him.*

Just shows to go ya, Rothstein. You never know. All it takes is one person in the right place, like Rachel, who likes the idea, makes some calls, and bingo, Canadian Film Museum, here we come!

ABBY   Terrific.

JULIUS   It's so funny, this business. They can't find the money to preserve it as a movie theatre, but the much bigger amount to rebuild it as a museum? No problem.

ABBY   Good.

JULIUS   You made a very good impression.

ABBY   Especially on Greenleaf.

JULIUS   Yeah, Greenleaf seems to like you.

ABBY   *Seems* to *like* me? He was all up on me! He was, like, *drooling*! It was *nauseating*!

JULIUS   You mean the flirting?

ABBY   You call that flirting? He was totally trying to do me!
          And I'm his student!

JULIUS   Your friend Megan didn't seem to mind him. She's in his
          class too, isn't she?

ABBY   Megan was even more hammered than Greenleaf, and
          she still thought he was pathetic.

JULIUS   I know, some of these older profs seem to think the stu-
          dents still find them attractive. But, you know, back in
          the eighties it was considered a perk of the job / that you
          could—

ABBY   Oh, stop it, stop it, stop it, you're making me sick!

JULIUS   Jeez, take it easy.

ABBY   I will not fucking take it easy! Even *you* were getting a
          little creepy, which I've never thought of you as. I saw
          you checking out Megan's cleavage.

JULIUS   I was not! I was checking out what's on both *sides* of her
          cleavage.

ABBY   You just think this is a big joke, don't you?

JULIUS   Hey, she's my type.

ABBY   She is *not your type*! Where do *you* get off having a *type*?
          You're *sixty-eight years old*! What is it with you old men!

JULIUS   What is it with *you*? There's no harm done, people got
         a little drunk and acted stupid and had a good time! It
         was a *party*, for Chrissake! Who elected *you* pope?

         ABBY *begins to weep.*

         Oy vey's mir. Abby. No, no, no. Come here. Come here.

ABBY   No. I don't want to talk about it. It's so stupid. It's too
         stupid a thing to cry over.

JULIUS   No it's not.

ABBY   It's not about the party.

JULIUS   Okay.

ABBY   So you don't even know what it is.

JULIUS   No, but I know you.

         A *brief silence.*

ABBY   I'm doing the laundry. Back home, a couple of months
         ago. And just like every time I do it, I go through every-
         body's pockets. And I always think, "Wouldn't it be
         funny if I found something," you know, "incriminating.
         Like in the movies." But I never do. Till this time. I find a
         piece of notepaper. Mauve. Folded. In his shirt pocket. I
         unfold it and it says, "Dear Davey," and something about
         how great the "encounter" was. And it is so totally not
         from Mom. So that night at dinner, when Mom's in the
         kitchen, I say, "I found this in the laundry," and I hand
         it to him. He turns white as a sheet. Scrambles to shove

it into his pants pocket as Mom comes in with dinner. Later, he comes to my room. He's all, "I'm sorry you had to find out that way." So I'm like, "You mean you're *lucky* I found out that way. And that it was me." And he's like, "Yeah, I didn't know you did the laundry." He didn't even know I do the laundry!

JULIUS   Do you know who she was?

ABBY   Not was. Is. It's still going on. It's a woman in his office. I've met her. Before. She's this tiny little elfin red-headed person in her forties. Black clothes, too much jewellery, I didn't like her much in the first place.

JULIUS   Is she Jewish?

ABBY   That makes it all right, if she's Jewish?

JULIUS   Of course not. I'm just curious.

ABBY   Yeah, actually, she's Jewish. So mazel tov, the Jews won this round.

JULIUS   Does Vanessa know?

ABBY   No. That's the worst part.

JULIUS   Oy, Abby. That is terrible.

ABBY   Yeah, well, you men just don't seem to know any better.

JULIUS   I was always bothered by their wedding. Civil ceremony in some room in city hall. It felt like all they wanted was a piece of paper so they could cohabit. When it's held together that thinly, I'm not surprised it's coming apart.

ABBY   What? Twenty-some years later? Because they didn't get married in a synagogue?

JULIUS   No, I don't know, / I just—

ABBY   Because he married a shiksa it's her fault he's screwing around? Are you blaming Mom for this?

ABBY starts to exit.

JULIUS   Of course not. This is David's fault. Come back here.

ABBY   No, I'm going to bed. So he didn't mention any of this on the phone, eh?

JULIUS   What do you mean? When?

ABBY   When you phoned him. Like you promised you would, the first week I got here. Oh, you didn't phone him? What a surprise. Next time you phone him you can give him shit for not keeping his promises.

She exits.

AUDIENCE SCENE: JULIUS ON HOCKEY

JULIUS   Now this hockey thing with Abby, this I never saw
coming. Might as well be honest, a lot of you already
know this, I've always had a cordial loathing for the
culture of hockey. My father Irving, aleveh sholem, who
would be so pleased and proud to be here today—he was
a huge fan, went to many a game—it was Montreal in
the fifties, for God's sake, the Habs in their prime—and
yet he never once took me, and then he would kvetch
at me about my not appreciating the great game. And I
never figured out the rationale behind this, then or after.
Sorry, Dad. And, sorry to the rest of you, I guess that's
a story without much of a resolution. He was a good
loving father, but this was one of those unresolved issues
that it seems all fathers and sons have between them.
One of those mysteries that we all leave behind us when
we go. Anyway, I developed a hatred for everything to
do with the game. So, of course, guess what turns out
to be Abby's greatest passion in life? At least until she
met Noah.

HOME FROM HOCKEY

Evening, October. ABBY *enters through the front door with her hockey gear, followed by* JULIUS.

ABBY Every time I looked up into the stands, you were sitting there looking thoughtful and profester-orial.

JULIUS I was trying to understand the rules.

ABBY Okay: rule number one, jump up. Whenever we make a good move, or just when everybody around you jumps up and yells, you jump up too. Instead of sitting there applauding politely, like somebody made a cogent point about *Rashomon* or something. I want to see some juice out there.

JULIUS Like the tall guy with the curly black hair?

ABBY Yeah, he was into it, eh?

JULIUS He was into *you.* Who is he?

ABBY His name's Noah Gideon. I never met him before. Megan introduced us after the game.

JULIUS I see him in shul every Shabbos.

ABBY Oh, yeah?

JULIUS Yeah. He's cute. Isn't he?

ABBY   You think?

JULIUS   Boy, *he* sure jumped up whenever you made a good move. *And* when you came out to the lobby after the game. Why, he was just jumpin' up all over the place, was our new friend Noah Gideon.

ABBY   You're just prejudiced. You like him 'cause he's Jewish.

JULIUS   Not quite. I like him because you deserve a boyfriend who treats you right, and Jews tend to treat their women right.

ABBY   You mean like Dad?

JULIUS   Okay, I'm prejudiced. You might have introduced me.

ABBY   I just met him myself. And there were a lot of people. Anyway, I did point you out. And he said, "So that's your grandfather! That asshole who sat there applauding like it was a lecture on *Rashomon*!"

JULIUS   He did?

ABBY   No, Rothstein, I just made that up, it's a joke.

THE MORNING OF THE UNVEILING

Morning. JULIUS *is getting dressed in his synagogue attire, including his plain yarmulke. Suddenly he stops as if interrupted and pays attention. Pause.*

JULIUS Hi.

Pause.

Listen, I apologize. I been in denial, how much I hurt you. I'm seeing that now, thanks to Abbeleh. Shit she's going through with David. God, she reminds me of you. More than David does. Maybe gender trumps generation, eh? He's more like me. Apparently.

Brief silence. He resumes dressing.

Anyway. She's waiting outside at the car, and I don't want to be late for you. You're gonna get a nice little crowd today. Your usual fans. It's warm for October. The headstone is beautiful. And I'll say you a nice kaddish. Honey?

A brief pause.

Next time, stick around a while.

He continues dressing.

DRESSED LIKE THAT

Evening. JULIUS is marking papers. ABBY enters from her room in a sexy Halloween costume. At first he doesn't look up.

ABBY   Happy Halloween!

JULIUS   I am so tired of the same old insights into the same old movies, over and over again. Course, the students always think this is fresh-minted stuff, / so I hate to—

ABBY   Yeah, sorry, Rothstein, but I gotta go. Trick or treat! Check it out!

JULIUS   *(sees her)* Holy shit. Where are you going?

ABBY   Halloween party! Catch ya later! Don't wait up!

            ABBY starts to exit.

JULIUS   Uh— Wait! Wait wait wait! Where's this party?

ABBY   The Red Porch. Bunch of guys in film and theatre. You know some of them.

JULIUS   Yeah, I know about the Red Porch. You got your phone?

ABBY   Always.

JULIUS   How are you getting home?

ABBY   A bunch of us have it all worked out. We're gonna get drunk and steal a police car. I'll take a cab home, Rothstein. I'll be fine.

JULIUS   These are all friends? These people you're partying with?

ABBY   Excuse me, hello, I thought we were dormmates. You've never grilled me like this before.

JULIUS   Well, frankly, you've never gone out dressed like this before.

ABBY   Oh, come on. My friends in res just step out the door of their room and there's a social life going on. I feel so cut off out here sometimes! I can't afford cabs, and the buses are so slow!

JULIUS   It's not that I don't want you to have a social life.

ABBY   You just don't want me going out dressed like a slut.

JULIUS   You're not dressed like a slut. Exactly. But I will say, Greenleaf would love that outfit.

ABBY   Ooh! Smooth move, Rothstein, but I am not changing!

JULIUS   Look, you want a social life, why don't you invite your friends here?

ABBY   Everybody really likes you, Rothstein, but, you know, there is kind of an age difference, after all. If they came here, we'd spend the evening talking about film.

JULIUS I'm not like that! I don't have to spend the evening talking film!

ABBY   No, *they* would. It's just different. You want them to come here and get drunk and noisy like we do at our parties?

> *A honk is heard coming from the street.*

There's my ride. Don't wait up. I'll see you in the morning.

> *She exits through front door.*

JULIUS Gai gezunterhait.

NOAH WAS AT THE PARTY

> *Late that night.* JULIUS *sleeps, with the lamp on and a student essay in his hand. Music plays quietly on the stereo.* ABBY *enters through the front door in her party outfit. She sees him, turns off the lamp, and takes the essay from his hand. Then she turns off the stereo. This wakes him up.*

JULIUS What? Oh. Hi. What?

ABBY   You fell asleep.

JULIUS Okay.

ABBY   You waited up for me. That's so sweet.

JULIUS I was marking.

ABBY   You can go to bed now. G'night.

          *She kisses him on his brow and crosses towards
          her room.*

JULIUS   Wait, how was the party?

ABBY   It was okay. Noah was there.

JULIUS   Oh, yeah?

ABBY   Yeah. We talked a little.

JULIUS   Did he tell you, he and I have now advanced to nodding
          to each other in shul?

ABBY   No, didn't mention it. He's Israeli. He's from Tel Aviv. He
          used to be a paramedic with the Israeli army. Here, he's
          a grad student in international development. He teaches
          first aid.

JULIUS   What's his sign? Favourite colour? Favourite ice cream?

ABBY   *(amused)* Shut up.

JULIUS   Sounds like you talked more than a little.

ABBY   Maybe. He was interested that the Loyalist Film Museum
          was my idea. Did you know there's a bunch of student
          groups who have their eye on the place too?

JULIUS   I'm not surprised, location and all. But too bad, the uni-
          versity bought it for us.

ABBY   Yeah, well, these guys are going after it anyway. They
           call themselves the Committee to Occupy the Loyalist.

JULIUS   "Occupy"! Nice.

ABBY   Interesting groups. Students with Disabilities, Scientists
           Against Cruelty to Lab Animals, the Canadian Alliance
           to Legalize Marijuana, the Student Communist Society—

JULIUS   The Communist Society? *Those* guys are still around?

ABBY   Well, different actual guys from the ones you knew.

JULIUS   I wouldn't be so sure.

ABBY   Anyway, they all moved into the same low-rent building,
           over the years, 'cause they had politics in common. And
           now it's getting torn down. So they're all crying perse-
           cution, and pressuring the university to rent them the
           Loyalist for cheap.

JULIUS   And how come Noah knows all this stuff and I don't?

ABBY   Oh, Rothstein, Twitter much? Word gets around.

JULIUS   You think these people have a chance?

ABBY   Noah thinks so.

JULIUS   Sounds like Noah could prove a useful source of
           information.

ABBY   He's not gonna go spying on these guys for you.

JULIUS   Fair enough. So didja get any action?

ABBY   Don't be crude! Maybe. He kissed me good night. And we're gonna Facebook each other.

JULIUS   Ah, courtship in our time. Well, I look forward to a friendly exchange of views with him about the Loyalist.

ABBY   Okay, then, I'll tell you one other group that wants the place. Students for Palestinian Rights. G'night, Rothstein.

    She kisses him on the head and exits.

JULIUS   *(alone)* Oh, shit.

JULIUS THE SLOB

    Daytime. November. JULIUS *is thumbing his cellphone.*

ABBY   *(off)* The first night I got here, didn't you say something about how you weren't really this much of a slob?

JULIUS   I'm not.

ABBY   *(off)* Oh, so the state of this kitchen is just an illusion? I feel better already.

JULIUS   Hey, we're both busy. Things pile up.

ABBY   *(enters)* You owe me a hundred and sixty-five bucks, which, you know, to me, that's a lot of money. I paid the utility bill. I saw it lying on the kitchen counter. Overdue. So.

JULIUS   Don't pay the utility! That's my responsibility!

ABBY   It was a week overdue.

JULIUS   That's my problem! I hate that! Do not pay my bills!

ABBY   Just don't leave it till they cut off our heat.

JULIUS   Don't be silly, I wouldn't do that.

ABBY   No? When did you say you'd call Dad? Back in September? It's November. Have you called him?

JULIUS   Will you drop this already? I will call him, and I will not leave us in the dark! Man, you can be a nag sometimes.

ABBY   Well then, you'll be glad to know that in two weeks I'm running away from home.

JULIUS   Oh, good.

ABBY   Just for the weekend, though. Ski club's organizing a trip.

JULIUS   Oh! Two weeks from this weekend?

ABBY   Yeah. Why?

JULIUS   I have a colleague coming into town, a doctor, Sidney Goldberg, who's a graduate, and comes back sometimes to lecture the students. Would your room be available for the weekend?

ABBY   I guess. If this doctor guy is tidier than you are.

JULIUS   Okay. Thanks. And I'll write you a cheque for the one sixty-five, and for God's sake, don't pay any more bills!

ABBY   What is your problem with that?

JULIUS   I just hate it when you take over my finances and stuff.

ABBY   I never did that before.

JULIUS   You, collectively. Women. Whom I live with. Both marriages, it turned into her nagging me about not paying the bills, and me feeling castrated. I don't know whether I was attracted to the same kind of woman each time, or whether all women are the same once you get to know them.

ABBY   Or maybe it's—

JULIUS   Anyway, I've got it down to a bumper sticker: Whoever I marry turns into my wife.

ABBY   Oh, you mean they both cleaned up after you? Nice.

    ABBY exits to the kitchen.

DR. GOLDBERG'S BRA

Evening. Early December. JULIUS *is once again marking papers.* ABBY *enters through the front door.*

ABBY   Hey! The skier is home from the hills!

JULIUS   Hey yourself! How was it?

ABBY   It was good. I'm gonna crash. I'll see you in the morning.

JULIUS   Okay. Tired, eh? Lots of skiing?

ABBY   Yeah, and I was up late last night.

JULIUS   Partying, eh?

ABBY   Actually, no. Mostly I talked with Mom on the phone. She's complaining that Dad seems more and more distant, for some strange reason.

JULIUS   Oh, shit.

ABBY   Yeah. But I'm not gonna tell her. That's Dad's job.

JULIUS   That's right.

ABBY   But it's hard to listen to, and it makes me really look forward to going home for Christmas. Anyway. Did your doctor friend show up?

JULIUS   Yes. And you'll find your room in perfect condition.
           Sidney says thank you.

ABBY   You guys have a nice visit?

JULIUS   Yes, thanks.

ABBY   Okay. I'm gonna crash.

           She exits.

           (off) You're right. The room is very nice.

JULIUS   Told you.

           He continues marking papers. A brief silence.

ABBY   *(off)* Rothstein?

JULIUS   Yeah?

ABBY   *(re-enters from bedroom)* There's a bra in my room.
           Which isn't mine.

JULIUS   *(reading)* Oh. Must be Dr. Goldberg's.

ABBY   Sidney Goldberg is into wearing women's underwear?

JULIUS   I should hope she is.

ABBY   Sidney Goldberg is a lady?

JULIUS   Every inch. Leave it on the table at the foot of the stairs,
           I'll mail it back to her.

ABBY   Uh huh.

        She exits to her room. Pause. She re-enters.

        Rothstein?

JULIUS *Yes...*

ABBY   It was in the bed. Under the sheets.

JULIUS So?

ABBY   So why would she get into bed first, and then take off
        her bra?

JULIUS Jesus, how should I know? Enough already with the bra.

ABBY   Okay.

        ABBY *exits, then re-enters.*

        Rothstein.

JULIUS You know, I think I've read this sentence five times now,
        and it's a godawful sentence.

ABBY   She gets up this morning. She makes the bed. She still
        doesn't see the bra?

JULIUS Fuck, I dunno! The sheets on your bed are all white and
        lacy, and it's a white lace bra, so maybe it just kind of
        (realizes what he's saying) blended in with—

        Beat.

ABBY produces the white lace bra.

ABBY   Good guess.

ABBY throws it at him.

JULIUS   Hey, careful!

ABBY   Of what? It's a lace fucking bra!

JULIUS   It's got those little *hooks*.

ABBY   You were doing it with this woman!

JULIUS   Trying to.

ABBY   In your *granddaughter's bed*?

JULIUS   It's the guest room, it's where she was sleeping anyway. So I didn't think it was / such a big—

ABBY   It's my room now! Do it upstairs in your own bed!

JULIUS   That's Phyllis's bed! Anyway, Sidney has trouble with stairs.

ABBY   What? How old is— How long has this been going on, anyway?

JULIUS   That's none of your business.

ABBY   For a while! Hasn't it!

JULIUS   It's none of your business.

Pause.

ABBY   Like, *years?*

JULIUS   Abby, this is something I don't think you'd understand.

ABBY   Oh, my God.

JULIUS   Phyllis knew.

ABBY   Oh, my God.

JULIUS   Marriages are compromises. Sometimes they require accommodations. Not everybody can be everything to the person they love.

ABBY   No kidding. I came here to get away from this shit. I should have known it runs in the family.

     ABBY exits.

AUDIENCE SCENE: BEFORE ABBY WAS BORN

JULIUS   The fact is, I was Abby's doting, devoted fan long before she moved in with me. Even before she was born. Literally. Couple of days before she popped, we're all having dinner and Vanessa says, "She's kicking!" and puts my hand on her belly. And I feel Abby doing a little aquatic tap dance, and I'm thinking, "Confident, assertive, yet somehow restrained, perhaps with a hint of irony— Yes, I like this girl, we're gonna get along fine."

He addresses one side of the imaginary audience.

I don't know if you remember that, Vanessa—

He searches the audience on the opposite side.

And, uh, David, wherever you—oh, there you are—I don't know if you, uh, remember that.

AFTER ABBY'S PARTY

Daytime. The morning after a big, boisterous party. The house is a mess: bottles, beer cups, pizza boxes, etc. The antique mirror is missing. ABBY *sleeps on the floor.* JULIUS *enters the front door in winter clothes and with a suitcase and laptop.*

JULIUS   Oh my God. *Abbeeey*!

ABBY   Oh, crap.

JULIUS   *Surpriiise*! *Zaaaydie's home*!

ABBY   You weren't gonna be back from Ottawa till tomorrow.

JULIUS   You weren't gonna throw a party.

ABBY   How come you're back so early?

JULIUS   How come you threw a party?

ABBY   *(looks around)* Oh, man. Worse than it looked last night.

JULIUS   Well, of *course* it's worse than it looked last night! You were *drunk* last night! The whole place is— Where's the mirror?

ABBY   Jesus. I don't know.

JULIUS starts looking in drawers, behind furniture, etc.

JULIUS   What the fuck happened to the bloody mirror? *(finds it)* Oh, my God.

He takes it out from where it was hidden, revealing that the glass has broken.

ABBY   Oh, my God.

JULIUS   Did you know about this?

ABBY   No!

JULIUS   Can you remember anything?

ABBY   Yes! I remember everything! I wasn't that drunk!

JULIUS   You didn't know somebody broke the mirror? And then *hid* it?

ABBY   No.

JULIUS   This mirror came over with Phyllis's grandmother.

ABBY   I know.

JULIUS   It survived the Nazis.

Silence.

So what happened to our no-parties rule?

ABBY Yeah, well, I kind of thought you threw that rule out the window with Dr. Goldberg.

JULIUS We left a bra in your bed. Your friends kind of trashed the whole house, Abby.

ABBY I'll pay for the mirror.

JULIUS Yes, you will, except it'll be David who pays for it.

ABBY Or I'll find out who did it, and they can pay for it.

JULIUS Fine. Of course, even if I can replace the glass, it won't be the same, will it. All the generations that were reflected in that glass, gone.

ABBY *Okay*! Holy fuck, Jesus Christ, I'm sorry my Nazi friends broke Bubbie Phyllis's fucking family heirloom *mirror*! You know what, if *Sidney Goldberg* had broken the mirror, you wouldn't give two shits!

JULIUS Well, yes I would, but it's my mirror!

ABBY Right! Everything in this house is yours! All that crap about how we're equal partners, we're housemates, it's bullshit! I am still just a guest in your house! That's why I do all the cleaning up, I always feel like I'm *imposing* on you! I didn't want to live here in the first place, you know. Dad kept pushing for it, 'cause he said you were so *lonely*, and I'd / be doing you—

JULIUS   Lonely? Why does he assume I'm lonely!

ABBY   I'd be doing you a *favour*—

JULIUS   You're not doing me a favour! *I'm* doing *you* a favour!

ABBY   Yeah, which is why I'm always cleaning up! Anyhow, it's not working. I am so outta here. I am getting out today. I'll stay at Megan's till exams are over and find my own place for next term, and when I come back after New Year's we won't even have to see each other.

JULIUS   What about this mess?

ABBY   You know what? I've done enough cleaning up after you, you can clean up this mess. I am so totally outta here!

JULIUS   Fine.

ABBY   *Fine*!

JULIUS   Fine!

> *She exits to her room.*

Damn.

PHONING DAVID

Evening. JULIUS *is on the phone.*

JULIUS   So it's down to you and this one other guy?... Well, mazel
tov, Daveleh... For beating out the rest of the competi-
tion... Well, it *could* matter, even if he gets it, couldn't it?
Like, next time?... I didn't say he's gonna get it, David.
I'm sure you're more than qualified for the promotion...
Oh? How much younger?... Oh. Well, still... Excuse me?
Is *what* why she moved out?... No, David, first of all I'm
not being passive-aggressive, and, second, she moved out
'cause she threw a wild party while I was out of town
and we had a big fight, didn't she tell you that?... That's
right, you called it, kiddo, we're at each other's throats,
just like you said we'd be, mazel tov... Hello?... Yeah, I
couldn't tell if the phone line's breaking up or you were
pausing. Okay, well, one more thing. She says you got
something going on with a co-worker?... So is this a fling,
or do you plan to break up with Vanessa, or what?...
Because Abby's about to spend three weeks with you
guys, and you can't make her spend them helping you
lie to her mother... Of course there will. You thought
you'd get through this without a shitstorm? Or did you
think you could keep it going forever? 'Cause you can't,
you know... What's that supposed to mean?... *Who* told
you?... *Phyllis?*... Okay. Well. Maybe you can, but believe
me, there's still a shitstorm, and, anyway, you pay a big
price. And so do they. And you go on paying it, long after.
So the sooner you tell Vanessa, or dump the redhead, or
both, the less shitstorm it's gonna be by the time Abby
gets there... Yeah, we're pissed off at each other; what,

this means I shouldn't care? Hello?... You're breaking up. Listen, get back to me with your decision. Keep me posted. Phone me, email me, Facebook, Facetime, Skype, tweet, whatever, we have so many ways to communicate, don't we?... Wrong, David, it is absolutely my business... Because you're making Abby collude in behaviour she doesn't approve of, by keeping it secret from her mother, and because Abby is— Hello? You still there? David?

Pause.

I've lost you.

Pause.

If you can still hear me: she's my grandkid.

He ends the call.

Act Two

AUDIENCE SCENE: ON THE SWING

ABBY When I was seven years old, we were at Rothstein's place during the summer—

JULIUS Once, when she was about seven, I was visiting the family in Victoria—

ABBY And he took me to the playground and we went on the swings.

JULIUS And I was pushing her on a swing.

ABBY And he started this silly joke.

JULIUS So I began this running gag that I used to use on David when he was little.

ABBY He started complaining that I kept coming back to him.

JULIUS   "I keep pushing you away—and you keep coming back!"

ABBY   I sort of forced a laugh, because I thought maybe he was genuinely annoyed.

JULIUS   She thought this was the funniest thing she'd ever heard.

ABBY   But our teacher'd been teaching us about gravity and momentum.

JULIUS   But then she surprised me.

ABBY   I got him to grab the chains so the swing would stop—

JULIUS   She told me to stop the swing—

ABBY   And I turned to him and said, "Don't you know swings are pendulums?" *(simultaneously with* JULIUS, *below)* And *he* said, "Rothstein. Love is a pendulum."

JULIUS   And *she* said, "Rothstein! Love is a pendulum!" Wisdom, from the mouths of babes.

PHONING ABBY

JULIUS at home, ABBY elsewhere. The house is tidier than it has been. The mirror is back in place, with new glass. JULIUS is phoning ABBY. She checks her phone and answers.

ABBY   Rothstein.

JULIUS   Rothstein. Hi again. Nice running into you.

ABBY   Yeah. Sorry, I had to go 'cause I was late for class.

JULIUS   Yeah, you said. What class?

ABBY   Why, you gonna check out my story?

JULIUS   No, silly, I'm just interested in what you're taking this term.

ABBY   Psych.

JULIUS   That's what you're taking, or you're psyching me out?

ABBY   Both.

JULIUS   Okay.

ABBY   So why'd you call?

JULIUS   Why did I *call*? Uh, because hi, this is your grandfather, and how are you, and when did you get back, and where are you living, and what other courses are you taking this term, and how was Christmas break, and would you like to come over for dinner some time.

ABBY I'm fine. I got back the day after New Year's, I'm staying on Megan's couch while I look for, you know, a room of one's own. You think *I* throw wild parties? You should see hers. What was the rest?

JULIUS Courses?

ABBY Right. Feminist literature, can't you tell? And psych, and anthropology, and the rest of that culture-of-languages course with Greenleaf.

JULIUS Good mix. How were things in Vicsnoria?

ABBY Cloudy and rainy.

JULIUS No, really? And the weather?

ABBY Yeah, that too. Dad finally told her.

JULIUS Ah!

ABBY Yeah. Greek tragedy. She's kicked him out of the house.

JULIUS She kicked him out! Jesus. So how do you, uh— Is this good news or, uh—

ABBY Oh, it's okay. It's a relief. At least it's out there. I stayed with Mom, who cried most of the time but made a good effort on Christmas Day. And I visited Dad, who is living in a *basement apartment* in *Esquimalt,* for God's sake.

Oh, and also the shit hit the fan at work, apparently. He says this thing with the redhead cost him the promotion. He's trying not to be bitter.

JULIUS   I'm so sorry. Did you have to play dreidel with the redhead?

ABBY   No, he spared me that. Though he wouldn't shut up about her winning little ways. She makes him feel young again. Which is weird, 'cause he looks older than ever. I took to making barf noises whenever he mentioned her.

     JULIUS is laughing.

It's not that funny.

JULIUS   I know. It's your unique delivery. Come over for dinner. Soon.

ABBY   Okay. Thanks. I will. I just have to sort out my schedule. I'll get back to you.

JULIUS   Okay. Still seeing Noah?

ABBY   More than ever.

JULIUS   Glad to hear it. Give him my best.

ABBY   I will. Thanks for calling, Rothstein.

JULIUS   Okay, bye.

ABBY COMES HOME

Late at night, January. Darkness. Doorbell. JULIUS enters in a bathrobe.

JULIUS   Rothstein?

ABBY   *(off)* Yeah.

       JULIUS lets her in. She is wet and cold and is carrying an overnight bag.

I'm so sorry.

JULIUS   Jesus, kid, you look like a drowned rat.

ABBY   I know. Look, I know how late it is, I'm really sorry to keep you up.

JULIUS   It's fine, it wasn't that late when you called.

ABBY   Thank you. Is my bed—um, is the guest room bed made?

JULIUS   Yeah.

ABBY   Okay. I'll just go straight to bed.

JULIUS   What happened with Megan?

ABBY   It didn't work out. She has this new boyfriend who's there all the time. Plus he's a douche. Tonight she accused him of hitting on me.

JULIUS   Was he?

ABBY   Yeah. They had this huge fight. I told her I shot him down, but that's not the issue. Anyway, I thought of crashing at Noah's, but we're not quite at that stage yet. So you got yourself a drowned rat. Sorry.

JULIUS   It's absolutely all right. Are you okay?

ABBY   No. I'm falling behind. Already. I got no place to study, it's—I'm *couch* surfing. I didn't know you can't get a dorm room in January. And also, even if I got one, they still charge for the whole year. Also my laptop's chosen this month to keep going out on me.

JULIUS   You could come back. Half your stuff is still here anyway.

ABBY   I know. I've thought about it, Rothstein. I dunno.

JULIUS   I been thinking about the housework. You were right. I was a better housekeeper before you moved in. I think I was taking advantage. I'm sorry. If you came back, I would do my share.

          He indicates the state of the house.

          See? Already.

ABBY   Yeah. Nice.

JULIUS   And you could even throw parties, as long as I'm here for them. I wouldn't spoil your fun. I'd even smoke weed and drink beer with the kids, I promise.

ABBY   *(amused)* Good sales job. Let me think about it.

JULIUS Okay. In the meantime, yeah, get some sleep.

ABBY   *(sees mirror)* Oh. You replaced the glass. I really tried to find out who did it, but nobody would own up. So I'll pay for it.

JULIUS Okay.

ABBY   You're right, though, it's not the same. Did you fill up the guest room with cartons and storage bins again?

JULIUS Take a look.

        ABBY exits to her room. Pause. She re-enters.

ABBY   It's like I just stepped out for a second.

JULIUS You think?

        Brief pause.

ABBY   Dad said you phoned him. A few days before I went. Did you tell him to tell Mom?

JULIUS Yeah.

ABBY   Thank you.

JULIUS You're welcome. Okay, also: when David said I was lonely? It's true. I was lonely.

ABBY   Make you a deal. I'll come back if I can finish Bubbie's dress.

      Pause.

JULIUS   It's not your style.

ABBY   It's not about the dress. Sometimes I just go in that room and remember our conversations. I dunno, I'd just like to finish it for her.

      Pause.

JULIUS   It's the sound. Of the machine. Whenever I heard that sound, I knew she was home, and reasonably contented for the moment. I don't know if I can listen to that sound again.

ABBY   How about if I just work on it when you're out of the house?

JULIUS   Well, that's silly.

ABBY   No it's not.

      Pause.

JULIUS   Okay.

      Pause.

      Okay.

ABBY   Okay. G'night, Rothstein.

JULIUS   G'night, Rothstein.

ABBY exits to her bedroom.

WATCHING A MOVIE WITH JULIUS

Evening. JULIUS and ABBY are eating pizza and watching a DVD together. There's exciting suspense-film music coming from the TV. ABBY is also doing homework on her laptop.

JULIUS   Okay, watch, nobody'd ever done this before Jerry did it. We're on Bob, running down Yonge Street, and now he heads in the door of the strip club.

The music turns into strip-club rock.

ABBY   Rothstein—

JULIUS   Strip club interior continuing, Bob sees the manager, and he says, "Where's Delilah," and the manager's *in* focus and the back of Bob's head is *out* of focus, manager points to the stage, Bob turns towards the camera, out of focus, sees her onstage—watch this!

ABBY   I'm trying to!

ABBY picks up the remote.

JULIUS   As he realizes she's a stripper, he literally *comes into focus*! Jerry was the first director ever to—

ABBY *pauses the movie.*

What are you doing? Don't do that!

ABBY   I want a new rule!

JULIUS I told you, I hate when you hit pause! It's a crime against cinema!

ABBY   And lecturing over the dialogue isn't?

JULIUS I'm trying to show you what he's doing!

ABBY   I can *see* what he's doing! I would like to hear what they're saying! And you won't let me turn on the subtitles either!

JULIUS That's even worse. Not to mention doing your homework at the same time.

ABBY   It's multi-tasking, it's something young people do. You wouldn't understand.

JULIUS Ageist! Hate crime!

ABBY   See, I thought this evening was gonna be about eating pizza and watching a movie and doing a little homework. I did not sign on for an illustrated lecture by Profester Rothstein.

JULIUS God, you sound like Phyllis.

ABBY   Oh, gee, I wonder why! You know your theories on why both wives acted the same? I got another one. It's living with you, Rothstein, turns us all into the same kind of biatch.

JULIUS Hey, I'm doing more housework.

ABBY Some. Anyway, I'm almost finished proofing my essay on Atwood, and then I'll give the movie my full—

Pause. She hits a few keys on the computer.

Oh, no. Wait. Not now, I'm nearly finished! *Fuck off*!

JULIUS What?

ABBY Shit! Shit shit shit! It's frozen. That's it. My computer has totally flerged.

JULIUS No!

ABBY Yeah. Totally. Screen's frozen.

ABBY *tries the mouse and keyboard.*

Nothing.

JULIUS Oh, that does suck.

ABBY Well, at least it warned me. I told you, it's been glitching for a couple of weeks. So I been backing everything up on the cloud.

JULIUS Good for you. So it could have been worse.

ABBY   Yeah. But I just lost the latest draft of this Atwood thing.
            And all my notes from my first aid course.

JULIUS   You're taking a first aid course?

ABBY   Yeah. From Noah. I told you, he teaches it for St. John
            Ambulance.

JULIUS   Specializing in mouth-to-mouth?

ABBY   Don't be crass.

JULIUS   Well, you can share my laptop, for now.

ABBY   Really? Oh, thank you.

            He hands his laptop to her as he speaks.

JULIUS   Download your backups onto it, and write down for me
            when you're going to need it. We'll figure out a sched-
            ule. You can log on separately or not, I don't care, I got
            nothing to hide.

ABBY   Rothstein, you are the shit. Thank you so much.

JULIUS   Thank you, honey, you're the shit too. And, mean-
            while, take yours to I.T.S. You did save your stuff on the
            Brazilian ladies?

ABBY   Yeah, thank God.

JULIUS   How's that coming?

ABBY   Greenleaf disputes my thesis. You think he's gonna dock me marks 'cause he disagrees with me?

JULIUS   Course not. It's a university, that's what it's about. What's he say?

ABBY   He says Aboriginal languages contain essential information about the environment. Based off of centuries of observation, record keeping, and study. So the rest of us need the knowledge encoded in the Saliguando language. I'm saying screw the rest of us, what have we ever done for the Saliguando people besides nearly wipe them out. If we did get their language back, we'd prob'ly just use it to finish off their environment anyway.

JULIUS   Good argument. I love hearing you evolve intellectually.

She's exploring JULIUS's *laptop.*

ABBY   I know, I'm a genius. Though it feels so stupid, sitting in this cushy place in Ontario, writing a paper about a dying culture, and bitching about my laptop. First World problems. But anyway, thanks for the loan. Wow. I shouldn't be surprised, but man, you got a shitload of stuff in here.

JULIUS   Course. Dating back decades. Anyway. Shall we resume?

ABBY   Sure.

JULIUS presses the remote and the movie soundtrack resumes. As he talks, ABBY *notices a puzzling file name, opens the file, and is horrified by what she reads there.*

JULIUS   Okay, just one other thing. It's brilliant how Bob literally comes into focus, realizing she's a stripper, but Jerry kind of spoiled it by combining it with a Hitchcock dolly zoom, which was—

He turns, sees her staring at the laptop screen, and pauses the movie.

What?

ABBY   What? Nothing. Sorry. What?

She closes the laptop.

JULIUS   You paying attention?

ABBY   Yeah!

JULIUS   Well, it was all too much at once. Here, lemme show you again.

He rewinds the movie.

ABBY   Okay!

AUDIENCE SCENE: A REAL PROFESSOR

JULIUS   One evening in Vancouver, when Abby was about five, David and Vanessa went out, and Phyllis and I babysat. Abby and I were watching her favourite cartoon show. Phyllis was in the kitchen. So I asked about the character with the beard and the glasses and the tweed jacket with the leather elbows.

ABBY   *(age five)* Professor Synapse. He's smart, 'cause he's a professor.

JULIUS   The stereotype seemed incomplete, so I asked why he wasn't smoking a pipe.

ABBY   There's no smoking in children's television, Rothstein.

JULIUS   *(to her)* Oh, of course.

(to AUDIENCE) I told her we knew a real live professor: me. She didn't believe me.

ABBY   Oh, Rothstein, you are not.

JULIUS   I told her I was a professor of film and media studies at a university. She didn't believe me.

ABBY   Faker.

JULIUS   I gave her my card.

JULIUS, now younger, hands ABBY a business card.

Here, let's sound out the name together.

ABBY   "Julius Rothstein," I know how to read your name.

JULIUS   Okay, smarty pants, look at the two big words underneath.

ABBY   A-s-s— That spells "ass"! *(guffaws)* It says you're an ass!

JULIUS   Uh, no, that word is "associate," don't pay attention to that, look at the second word. P-r-o...

ABBY   Fessor. Professor. You can't be a professor. You don't have a beard.

JULIUS   Plenty of professors don't have beards. There's a lot of lady professors, and most of them don't have beards. *You* could be a professor.

ABBY   No.

JULIUS   What do you want to be?

ABBY   I don't know.

JULIUS   Anything but a professor?

ABBY   Yeah.

JULIUS   Why?

ABBY   Don't like the clothes.

JULIUS   You got a point there.

AFTER THE RALLIES

> *Early evening, February. JULIUS enters through the*
> *front door and removes his winter clothing, includ-*
> *ing his birthday toque. He carries a placard.*

JULIUS   I have to say, that other group was the dumbest-looking protest I've seen in some time.

> *ABBY enters and removes her winter clothes.*

ABBY   Wow, Rothstein, you mighta warned me how cold it gets in February! I been here at Christmas before, but it was never like this.

JULIUS   All the worst excesses of the Occupy movement. The white boys with dreadlocks, / the finger-waving—

ABBY   Rothstein, it's been / a long day—

JULIUS   And the placards! "Human Rights, not Film Nights"! "People Before Pomposity"—what the hell does that mean? What's pompous about a film museum? Who's it for, if not people? Oh, and "Warmth and Shelter, Not William Shatner."

ABBY   Well, your signs were pretty lame too. "Honour Canadian Cinema." Yawn.

JULIUS   And, nice as it was to see you and Noah there, did you have to stand among the stoners and hacky-sackers and misspelled placards? People might have thought you were part of the Occupy crowd.

ABBY   Oh. Sorry.

JULIUS I had no idea how insulting they'd be. I don't appreciate being labelled part of the elitist, artsy, snob side of the issue.

ABBY   You're not being labelled! Sorry, but that's the side you're on! You can build your museum anywhere in Canada. The only place they can put these campus groups is on this campus.

JULIUS It's a big campus!

ABBY   Also, I gotta say, you were being really immature today. The shouting match with the girl in the wheelchair, what the fuck, Rothstein? Sometimes I think you're the grandkid in this relationship. I know you're always saying people should be free to argue, / but sometimes you—

JULIUS Yes. It's what universities are all about. Socratic, Talmudic, free and open debate.

ABBY   Okay. Noah and I *are* part of the Occupy crowd. Noah is the chairman of Students for Palestinian Rights.

JULIUS You're kidding.

        Pause.

        You're not kidding.

ABBY   No.

JULIUS   This shul-going Israeli Jew supports the Palestinians?

ABBY   Yeah. And he's not the only Jew in the group. It's not
            anti-Israeli. It's pro-human rights.

JULIUS   Do not lecture me about this! How long have you known
            this man's politics?

ABBY   Since the Halloween party.

JULIUS   Why have you not told me?

ABBY   'Cause I was glad you liked him.

JULIUS   Ah, but you've told him *my* politics, haven't you.

ABBY   Yes! I did! 'Cause I knew he'd like you anyway! 'Cause
            he can *respect* people he disagrees with. But I knew if I
            told *you his* politics, then I'd never hear the end of it. I
            have homework to do.

            She starts to exit.

JULIUS   And you?

            ABBY *stops.*

            Do you belong to this Students for Palestinian Rights
            thing?

ABBY   Yes. Yes, I joined three weeks ago, just after I got back.
            And, you know what, for three weeks now I've been

afraid to tell you. 'Cause I knew you were gonna make my life miserable when you found out. And that really pisses me off. But guess what, Rothstein, love is love and there's fuck all you can do about it.

JULIUS *Love* we're talking now?

ABBY Yeah, love we're talking now, you and I are gonna love each other whether we agree about this or not. And I'm not quitting on Noah either. Or the group. So you got a decision to make. 'Cause this guy's around for the foreseeable. You gotta decide whether to accept him, or whether the Palestine thing is a deal breaker.

JULIUS Yes.

ABBY Yes what?

JULIUS Yes, you're right, I have a decision to make.

A brief pause, then she exits.

PHONING VANESSA

ABBY *(on the phone, daytime)* Yeah, he likes him. Everybody likes him. He just has a problem with his politics... *Zaydie*, with *Noah's* politics. Well, and vice versa, but Noah doesn't make me suffer for it... No, otherwise we're getting along better now. Mostly. He's doing more house-work... Where do you get this that he's taking Daddy's side! If anything, he's been taking *your* side! Did you even know it's because of him that Daddy finally told you?... Oh, come on, you seriously wish Daddy hadn't told you?... All right, then... Yeah, true, he did it for me, so I guess he's been taking *my* side... You do so: it's that Daddy's being an asshole, and, at least for now, you're better off without him... Uh huh... Uh huh... Uh huh... I know, it really sucks, but— Uh huh... So anyway, Mom, I'm getting back on track at school and Noah and I are doing great, and— Uh huh, well, see, I'm still hoping they're *not* all the same... Uh huh... Uh huh... Uh huh, so, listen, have you considered lesbianism?... Sorry, okay, I was just trying to— Yes, Mom, some of my best friends too, I wasn't making fun of— Yes, Mom, we were talking men... Uh huh... Uh huh... Uh huh...

THE GUY WHO KILLED HIMSELF

JULIUS and ABBY are having breakfast. JULIUS peruses the newspaper.

JULIUS   Hey, here it is. *(They both look at the paper.)* Well, of course the picture's gonna be the sexy kids on your side instead of us old farts.

They read together.

ABBY   Yeah, but so is the story.

JULIUS   God. It is. It's like it was all your side's idea, and we're just a paragraph at the end.

ABBY   That's not fair to your side. It should be equal coverage.

JULIUS   Thank you. And in our bit at the end, the only person he quotes is Rachel. I gave this guy ten minutes of good stuff! See, this is why the newspaper as an institution is dying out.

ABBY   *(amused)* 'Cause they don't quote *you*?

JULIUS   Exactly. *(turns page)* Oh shit. I forgot about this. We've had another suicide.

ABBY   What?

JULIUS   Third-year chem major, found dead in his dorm yesterday.

ABBY   Oh my God. Oh, that's awful! That is so awful.

JULIUS   Yeah. Major cause of death among post-secondary students.

ABBY   Jesus. You think maybe he was gay, and other people were / giving him a—

JULIUS   No. Reportedly he was not gay.

ABBY   You knew about this?

JULIUS   Yeah, I heard last night. Anyway, that's high-school stuff, gay kids being bullied. We're much more sophisticated. This guy was the classic university model. Friendless, solitary nerds who put all their energy into schoolwork but start to flunk out anyway, and because they've turned their backs on everybody they don't know how to ask for help. This poor shmuck fit the pattern perfectly.

ABBY   Jesus, Rothstein, why don't you get pissed off at the guy,
            that'll help.

JULIUS   This kid was young and healthy and had options.

ABBY   It's a waste, of course it is; I know that.

JULIUS   Yeah, well, some people would rather live! Okay? Some
            people would rather live but they have to face the fact
            that they might die anyway.

ABBY   Uh—what are you saying?

            Brief pause.

JULIUS   Last March, I had a minor heart attack.

ABBY   Oh!

JULIUS   Oh, don't give me that, Rothstein. I don't need your pity.

ABBY   No, it wasn't pity, I just— Nothing. Never mind.

JULIUS   Stop it with the doe eyes. I'm just as alive as you are, and
            someday you'll be just as dead as I'm gonna be someday.
            Right?

ABBY   Right.

JULIUS   It was very minor. I was lucky. My doctor called it a
            warning. That's when I quit smoking, started exercising
            and took to eating this cardboard cereal. Don't tell David.
            I'll tell him when I'm ready. But what I'm *saying* is, some
            people would so much rather live that they'll give up a

hell of a lot to do so. Like cigarettes, like alcohol, except for one glass of red wine every Friday night, which I select very carefully—and remember the first night you got here, we casually had a beer?

ABBY   Yeah.

JULIUS I had saved up for that beer.

ABBY   I'm honoured.

JULIUS You should be. I've given up my favourite Jewish cooking— What else? Well, there's, oh, I dunno, *marijuana*— You know when I said I would drink beer and toke up with your friends if you came back? I was lying— There's a grad student who offered me some *acid*, not doin' *that* any more—

ABBY   You did acid?

JULIUS Oh, acid did me, baby. And you? Psychedelics, much?

ABBY   Never. Never never never.

JULIUS Fair enough. But anyway, that's over too. And so here I sit munching on cardboard like an alter kacker. So, yeah, life's a tiny bit less fun these days. But still, you know, at least it's life.

ABBY   Yes. Okay.

JULIUS Which, by the way, is why I don't need you hocking me over Sidney Goldberg, one of my few remaining pleasures.

ABBY   Haven't said a word about her since December. Anyway,
              it seems to be working, eh?

JULIUS   On and off. Cialis helps. Mind you, I'm also on prostate
              medication, which isn't / exactly—

ABBY   No, Rothstein, too much info, I meant your *regimen*. For
              your *health*. All this renunciation seems to be getting you
              results.

JULIUS   Oh! Oh, God, yeah. I started less than a year ago, and
              already I'm still alive.

ON THE SCREENING OF *LOW VISIBILITY*

              Late afternoon, February. ABBY *is at her own laptop on
              the dining room table, with papers scattered around.*

ABBY   *(calls out to* JULIUS*)* Hey. I'll be outta here in a few minutes
              and then I'll set the table. You're making your famous
              meat loaf, right?

              JULIUS *enters.* ABBY *sees his face.*

              I'm sorry. You still bummed about the Loyalist?

JULIUS   You should have asked me.

ABBY   Asked you what?

JULIUS   You broke your own rule. What happens at home stays
              at home.

ABBY   Oh. Wait. I'm not sure what you're talking about.

JULIUS   *Low Visibility.*

ABBY   Oh. *Low Visibility* didn't happen at home. It's a movie.
           It's been out there in public.

JULIUS   Was this you guys celebrating the Loyalist? A victory
           party? Couple dozen film students eating pizza and
           laughing at my movie?

ABBY   Nobody in our group was celebrating. We all knew you'd
           be disappointed.

JULIUS   Well, your timing couldn't have been better. Way to rub
           my nose in it.

ABBY   Oh, come on, Rothstein, nobody knew they were going to
           hand down the decision this week. Did *your* guys know?

JULIUS   No.

ABBY   Neither did our guys. We planned the screening, and then
           we heard the student groups got the building, and then
           we decided to go ahead with the screening.

JULIUS   It's the end of an era.

ABBY   I know.

JULIUS   End of two eras. The Loyalist, and any shred of cred I
           may have had with the students.

ABBY   That's not true.

JULIUS   Please. Everybody has now seen the failure that was my
         one and only feature film.

ABBY   Nobody thought it was a failure. Everybody loved it.
         Including me.

JULIUS   It's an honest, well-meant, miserable failure.

ABBY   Bullshit. All my life I've wanted to see that movie. Dad
         is so proud of you for making it, / but I'd never—

JULIUS   He— What? Really? He is?

ABBY   He talks about it all the time. But I'd never seen it. There's
         nowhere to download it, and I ask for it in video stores
         but they never have a copy.

JULIUS   Doesn't that tell you something?

ABBY   Not really, no. But then a few weeks ago, I found the
         copy you had hidden away here, in the basement, with the
         other old videotapes. So Megan books the film depart-
         ment's VCR, and she tells her housemates, and they tell
         their friends, most of which are your students and all of
         which adore you, / by the way—

JULIUS   Not all of them.

ABBY   Well, the ones who don't adore you didn't show up, okay?
         And it was *still* crowded.

JULIUS   Oh, God—

ABBY   And there was this huge applause at the end. And *every-body* said how *moving* it was. You and I might be biased, but those are film students, you notice them raving much about other people's work? And oh my God, the *actors* you had!

JULIUS   Yeah, good cast.

ABBY   "Good cast"? It's like a *Who's Who* of Canadian stars! Everybody was knocked out!

JULIUS   Why didn't you ask me first? I coulda been there and explained the parts that don't work. Which is most of it.

ABBY   I knew you wouldn't let me show it.

JULIUS   Aha.

ABBY   Out of false modesty. Or not wanting to look like a show-off.

JULIUS   It is none of the above. It is profound shame.

ABBY   Everybody asked me why you never made another one. I tried to tell them about the tax shelters and so on, but the film students already know that stuff, and I didn't explain it right.

JULIUS   It's not just that.

      Pause.

      I always felt like I didn't feel enough pain over Hannah's death. Everybody says, oh, car crash, you were both twenty-five, how awful. But it was—the awful thing about it was, it wasn't awful enough. I was at home, I got the phone call, I went to the hospital, and by the time I got there she was dead. They just came out and told me. I didn't have to view the body or anything. And I was shocked, and I was sad, but I kept waiting for the big, you know, the big meltdown, the big traumatic freak-out, and it just—never happened. I was suddenly busy with who do I tell, and how do I tell them, and then all the friends and mishpocheh gathered round, and the rabbi, and it was all about funeral arrangements, and the shiva—and then the next thing I know, I'm living alone in the apartment, I'm a bachelor again, and it's like, okay, that's over, now what do I do with my life? Not, "My life is ruined," just, "Okay, what now?" And I realized, I missed something. I was supposed to fall apart. Where was that moment when I was supposed to feel like I couldn't go on? So I thought, maybe this proves I didn't love her enough. So that's why I started the screenplay. I thought if I went through the whole thing again, but fixing it, adjusting it, helping it make more sense by turning it into art, then maybe I could trigger the feeling I should have had in the first place. But of course as I worked on the damn thing, it took on a life of its own, suddenly it was about all the thousands of details, and I was making a movie. And that grief I was supposed to have, it never arrived. Then when the movie came out, all the critics said it was this great, rough-hewn, artless, naked representation of my anguish over my dead wife, which was their way of cutting me some slack 'cause it wasn't really very well-made. And gradually I came to see the whole movie as a big, self-serving lie. Making people think I'd suffered like the guy in the movie. And exploiting Hannah's memory to do it.

ABBY   But to make good art that's about pain, do you have to really feel all the pain?

    Pause.

JULIUS   Good question. But I don't know and I don't care. My point is, I already made a movie that said, "Poor me, my wife died, I'm in hell," and it was bullshit. When Phyllis died, hey, no problem, that feeling hit me just fine. I got it. Thanks a lot. Careful what you wish for. This time, no need to make a movie to figure out what I felt. And anything with lower stakes than that, like your dear *Scarborough Bluffs*, why the fuck should I bother? But anyway, you owe me an apology. I should have been there. Or at least known about it.

ABBY   Okay. I apologize.

JULIUS   Thank you. I forgive you. I'll start dinner.

    He starts to exit to the kitchen.

ABBY   Sorry about the Loyalist, too. I mean, it's too bad it couldn't work out for both sides.

    JULIUS stops.

JULIUS   Well, that's politics. No, all right, that hurts too. However, your idea lives on, Rothstein. The museum committee's gonna look for another building.

ABBY   Great. Good.

JULIUS   Still, you know, I do have this urge to go out, the night before they start the renovation, and just spray-paint the whole outside of the old darling. Tag the bejeezus out of her.

ABBY   Are you going to?

JULIUS   Course not. My inner nineteen-year-old street-fighting man is in here yelling, "Do it, you chickenshit asshole!" But I'm sixty-eight. So I'm going in the kitchen and make my famous meat loaf.

    Brief pause.

You know something? You're the only person I've ever told that to. How I felt after Hannah's death. I never even told Phyllis.

    He exits to the kitchen.

ABBY, AFTER SHUL

    Morning, springtime. JULIUS *and* ABBY *enter through the front door,* JULIUS *dressed for synagogue.*

ABBY   Oh, come on, say it. You know you're dying to.

JULIUS   What?

ABBY   "With me, she won't go to shul. But Mr. Students for Palestinian Rights, him she'll go to shul with."

JULIUS   I was glad to see the two of you there, for whatever reason. Was I not cordial to you both?

ABBY   Totally.

JULIUS   Did I argue about Palestine?

ABBY   You said not one word on Palestine.

JULIUS   Course not, it's Shabbos. However, I've decided to friend him on Facebook. So tonight, when Shabbos is over, the cyberbullying begins.

ABBY   Oh, really? Good luck with that, Rothstein, lemme know how that works out for you.

JULIUS   I ask you, Rothstein! Did I say, "Mazel tov, Noah, you may be a traitor to Israel, but you got Abby to shul?" No I / did not say that.

ABBY   Rothstein! He is not a / traitor to—

JULIUS   And did I add that the glow on your face looks like he got you there by means of a good old Shabbos morning shtup beforehand? No, I did not say that!

ABBY   All right, now that's over the line!

JULIUS   Course it's over the line, that's why I didn't say it!

ABBY   (amused) You are such an asshole.

JULIUS   Yes, I am, but the most important question / is—

ABBY   Rothstein, that's / enough—

JULIUS   The most important question is, did you feel obliged to
         say words you didn't believe in?

         Brief pause.

ABBY   No.

JULIUS   Good. So come any time. No obligation. Just sit. As
         you may know, we Jews don't proselytize. Unlike some
         religions, with all due respect to them, but we don't go
         looking for converts. We don't even make it easy to get
         in. Women have to take a ritual bath, and men have to,
         never *mind* what.

ABBY   I know.

JULIUS   My point being, you're already in. You wouldn't have to
         do anything. If you ever wanted to come back.

ABBY   You're proselytizing.

         Beat.

JULIUS   Or don't. Go with Buddhism. Go with nothing. Go with
         God. Okay, Rothstein?

ABBY   Okay, Zaydie.

JULIUS   But, you know: always welcome. With or without
         Superjew.

ABBY   I might come back, if you promise not to call him Superjew.

JULIUS   Too late.

AUDIENCE SCENE: OBITUARY DRAFT

ABBY   One time when we were living together, my laptop crashed and I borrowed his. And I found something in his computer called "Obituary Draft." I'd like to read from it.

"Julius Rothstein set out to do great things for Canadian culture. And he almost did. But by his own assessment, he was one of the many who never quite got there. However, he was satisfied that he made a modest contribution, if only through his teaching. Even if he never did achieve the greatness he dreamed of, he felt, towards the end, that he did manage to achieve goodness. And in this corrupt, polluted, overheated world, maybe that too is an achievement."

I found that just a couple of months before his second, and last, heart attack.

DISHONESTY AND ATONEMENT

Late afternoon, spring. ABBY *is typing on her cellphone.*
JULIUS *enters from front door with the mail.*

JULIUS   Hey.

ABBY   Hey.

JULIUS   *(gives her a large envelope)* Something for you, from the
university.

ABBY   Oh, yeah? Thanks.

JULIUS   And here's the utility bill. Which I will pay by the due
date, which is March tenth, thank you very much.

ABBY   *(opening envelope)* Sweet. You haven't forgotten about
dinner tonight, right?

JULIUS   Nope. Copper Kettle. You, me, Noah, Megan, student
radicals from all sides, celebrating tomorrow's disem-
bowelling of the Loyalist. How could I forget.

ABBY   We are not *celebrating* it. I thought you were kind of
over this.

JULIUS   I am, it's not that. It's nothing, it's just— Phyllis's birthday
is Tuesday. Don't mind me.

ABBY   Oh. I'm sorry. Of course, you're gonna feel— *(stares at
the paper)* Just a second. Ohmygod. What the fuck?

JULIUS   What?

ABBY   It's from Greenleaf. "Dear Abigail. I regret to inform you that you may be guilty of an act of academic dishonesty."

JULIUS   What?

ABBY   "Enclosed please find your essay, 'Dead Language, Living Speakers: The Decline of the Saliguando Language of Brazil.' It appears to demonstrate a very different writing style from your previous essays. Please contact me as soon as possible. Sincerely, Terence Greenleaf."

She takes the essay out of the envelope.

JULIUS   Oops.

ABBY   Whaddaya mean, "Oops"? *(reads)*

JULIUS   Well, when you were using my laptop, I started reading it, and I found some grammatical errors, and then I was hooked on correcting them. Couldn't stop.

ABBY   You rewrote this whole paragraph!

JULIUS   It was unclear. I meant to tell you, but I forgot.

ABBY   "Be that as it may"? I would never write, "Be that as it may"!

JULIUS   You're supposed to read them over before you submit them.

ABBY   Don't put this on me! I read it over! Then you got your hands on it! *Then*, I *submitted* it!

JULIUS   You're right. I'm really sorry. I'll call him in the morning. I'll tell him it was my fault, you didn't even know about it.

ABBY   Can't you call him now?

    JULIUS sighs.

Don't you dare sigh! Don't you dare! You got a lot of chutzpah, you know that?

JULIUS   You know what, I think I'll call him now.

    As he gets the phone, he looks up the number and punches it in.

I just got carried away. It's kind of an OCD thing. From years of correcting essays. I leave them spattered with what looks like red ink, but it's my heart's blood. I can't stop myself.

(into phone) Terence! Julius... I'm good, thanks. Listen: about Abby's essay, the academic dishonesty thing?... You were right, there's a different style, 'cause we were sharing a laptop and I did some rewrites on it. However, she didn't know about them, and she submitted it thinking it was all her own work... Yeah, well, you know me. Anyway, it's entirely my fault. Call off your dogs. She'll send you the essay as she wrote it. I can also give you a written note on letterhead, if you want...

    ABBY *stands with her ear next to the phone.*

Okay, good... You're right, I'm sure I *didn't* improve it much... Yes, she *is* very good.

Greenleaf says something that offends them both.

ABBY   *(crossing away)* Oh, for God's sake.

JULIUS Terence, you're talking about my grandkid. You're talking about a student. That's sexual harassment... Yes, *of her, to me*, don't be obtuse! What?... Okay, fine, she'll send you the essay, g'bye.

He ends the call.

Well, I tried.

ABBY   Thank you, Rothstein.

JULIUS I'm sorry, Abby.

ABBY   Oh, he's a jerk.

JULIUS I'm sorry for tampering with your paper. For missing your bus. For the messy house. For the bra in the bed. For the fight over the party. For not raising David better. For losing Phyllis. I'm sorry I took away your bubbie.

ABBY   *You* didn't take / away my—

JULIUS Yes I did. It's my fault she died. I know, people always think / that, but—

ABBY   Oh, Zaydie, it is not!

JULIUS   She was depressed. Officially. Clinically. That's what brought on the heart attack.

ABBY   I know, / but—

JULIUS   And she was depressed 'cause I didn't give her all of myself. She needed me, but I wasn't there for her. Please forgive me.

ABBY   I'm not the one to do it.

JULIUS   No, but I need forgiveness right now, and she's not here, and frankly you could use the practice.

   ABBY hugs him.

ABBY   Rothstein, you are so full of crap. Didn't give her all of yourself. Who would *want* all of your self? She had about as much of your self as she could handle. I get about half of your self, and it's fucking exhausting.

JULIUS   Great, I feel better already.

ABBY   Are you saying your thing with Dr. Goldberg was enough to kill that woman? All she told me was, there was stuff you were doing that she wasn't crazy about. I thought it was drugs. It sounds like she didn't even care that much.

JULIUS   Jesus, okay, you can stop forgiving me.

ABBY   It's not that she didn't love you. But she was caught up in her own shit. Her job at the hospital, her own health, Dad and Mom, who were fighting long before the redhead—and frankly, not so much was about you. So mazel tov. You're off the hook.

She kisses his cheek and exits. Thinking about this, he sits in his chair.

PHYLLIS'S DRESS

An hour or so later. JULIUS *is asleep in the chair. From off, the sound of the sewing machine.*

JULIUS   *(in his sleep)* Phyllis?

ABBY   *(off, as machine stops)* Sorry! I was just so close to being finished, and I wanted to wear it to the dinner.

JULIUS   What?

ABBY   *(off)* The dress.

JULIUS   What dress?

ABBY *enters wearing Phyllis's dress.* JULIUS *opens his eyes.*

Oh, my God. Look at you. You look so much like Abby.

ABBY   Zaydie? Are you okay?

JULIUS   What? Abby. Oh. Right. She was just here. She was— Oh, my God.

> JULIUS *seems as if he's about to weep.*

ABBY   Oh, Zaydie, I'm sorry, I didn't mean to upset you. I wasn't / thinking—

JULIUS *(happily)* Oh, you look so beautiful, Rothstein. You look just like your bubbie. *(gets up)* Come here. I'm okay, come here. Let's look at the two of us.

> JULIUS *puts an arm around* ABBY. *They look in the antique mirror with its new glass.*

Oy, gottenu.

ABBY   What? Come on, we look cute together.

JULIUS I don't know, maybe it's the contrast with young, beautiful you—maybe it's this unforgiving new glass—but I look as old and tired as I feel. I'm not happy, Rothstein. In case you hadn't noticed. I'm tired of teaching, I'm scared of retirement—I'm realizing that all our friends were Phyllis's friends—and frankly I don't feel like I've done much with my life.

ABBY   How can you tell?

> *Beat.*

JULIUS You got a point. You can't count the house at your own funeral, can you.

ABBY   Not that we know.

JULIUS   Even so. Do you mind if I bail on this dinner? I'm not feeling too great. I wanted to show I'm a good sport about the Loyalist, but I'm not up for it.

ABBY   It's just a quiet, casual dinner. I do wish you'd come. The kids are looking forward to it.

JULIUS   I really don't want to, honey. I'm sorry.

ABBY   Okay, then, I have to tell you. We been planning a little after-dinner surprise.

JULIUS   Oh, no. What?

ABBY   You know when you said you wanted to go down the night before the renovations? And vandalize the Loyalist?

JULIUS   Yeah...

ABBY   Well, a bunch of us have got together and we're kind of gonna do that for you.

JULIUS   What are you doing to the Loyalist?

ABBY   Come on. Please. Everybody wants to see you.

JULIUS   All right. All right. I'm just flowing with the go here.

At the front door she puts his birthday toque on him. They exit together.

VANDALIZING THE LOYALIST

> *A parking lot by the Loyalist. Night. JULIUS and ABBY,*
> *JULIUS wearing the toque, sit on folding chairs and*
> *watch as film footage is projected over their heads*
> *onto an unseen wall.*

JULIUS   This is so far out, Rothstein!

ABBY   You like?

JULIUS   I love it! Where did you *get* these clips? Even *I've* never seen some of this stuff!

ABBY   We have our ways.

JULIUS   And nicely cut together. Good editing. Now *this* is how you vandalize a building!

ABBY   You said it never had a final screening. So this is the final screening.

> *ABBY looks at her cellphone, reads a text.*

JULIUS   On the outside. Brutiful.

> *The projection stops.*

ABBY   They're changing DVDs. Do you want to say a few words?

JULIUS   Oh, God, yes.

ABBY *gives him a microphone. He stands. A spotlight finds him.*

Good evening, fellow moviegoers! I'm Julius Rothstein from the university film department!

Some applause, cheering.

Thank you! And I can't think of a better way to celebrate this beautiful old building as she embarks on the next stage in her career. She's gonna get a nice jolt of energy in her old age from housing these exciting groups of young people. And believe me, our own committee's fight to build a Canadian film museum is not over!

More cheers. JULIUS *stops, holds his chest.*

Sorry. Wait a second.

Pause.

Earlier tonight, my friend Noah Gideon told me our committee members will always be honoured guests in the Loyalist. And, in return, when we open that museum, whenever, wherever, all of you new tenants at the Loyalist will be welcome to come check it out.

Cheers.

Are we ready? I think we're ready. We're going to see some more of these great clips from Canadian feature films. Here we go.

HEART ATTACK

Later that evening. JULIUS *and* ABBY *come in through the front door,* JULIUS *breathing a bit heavily.*

JULIUS   God, I'm still—feeling a little—overwhelmed.

ABBY   You okay?

JULIUS   Yeah, yeah, sure, I'm just—it's been a big day for mixed feelings. Listen, is Noah pissed off with me?

ABBY   No! He really appreciated it. He said you were a real mensch about it. Why?

JULIUS   I invited him back here for a drink. Twice.

ABBY   Oh. He thought you and I should be alone together.

JULIUS   We don't have enough time alone together? I thought our problem was too *much* time alone together.

ABBY   Zaydie, I have something to tell you. I'm going to take some time off from university.

JULIUS   What?

ABBY   Noah and I are going to Israel for a year or two. Maybe longer. To work.

JULIUS   You're dropping out?

ABBY   Maybe just for a while.

JULIUS   Honey, don't drop out now! I have it on good authority
         you did really well this year.

ABBY   I know I did. But Noah wants to go home to Israel.
         And today just confirmed everything I been thinking.
         Greenleaf's academic dishonesty bullshit, and all this
         fuss over the Loyalist—those film clips were fun, but,
         I'm sorry, to me it was just a movie theatre. So tonight I
         told him I've decided. I want to be doing something that
         matters. More. To me.

JULIUS   In Israel.

ABBY   Uh, well, specifically, in the West Bank. We want to work
         with the Palestinians. And last week I got an invitation
         to coach hockey at a Palestinian high school!

JULIUS   *(clutches his chest)* Oh, my God, I'm having a heart
         attack.

ABBY   Oh, please, that's not funny. You are not having a heart
         attack!

JULIUS   I think I'm gonna puke.

ABY   Stop being so dramatic!

JULIUS   No. Abby. I recognize this. I'm having a heart attack.

         He stands, knocks over a chair.

ABBY   What?

        ABBY *stands up, holds him.*

JULIUS   Chest pain, dizziness, left arm tingling—

ABBY   Oh, Jesus. Sit down.

        ABBY *helps* JULIUS *sit, takes out her phone, and hits 911.*

JULIUS   Chest pain increasing. Oh my God. On top of everything else today! *(He starts to laugh.)*

ABBY   *(into phone)* Ambulance... Two four three Earnscliffe Avenue... Sixty-eight-year-old man with chest pain, tingling in the left arm, nausea... Yeah, he used to, a lot, but he quit this year... Conscious... Yeah, a minor one, a year ago... Listen, are they on their way or what?... Okay, good. The front door's unlocked, tell them to just come in. Do I leave the phone on?... No, he's awake, he's hanging in... Okay.

    (to JULIUS*)* They're on their way. The thing to do now is try and relax. Stay calm. Maybe you shouldn't be laughing.

JULIUS   I know. How silly of me. *(laughs)*

ABBY   Can we loosen this shirt?

        ABBY *starts trying to remove* JULIUS*'s shirt.*

JULIUS   You did this—on purpose—told me you're gonna run off with Noah so I'd have a heart attack—so you could impress me—with the first aid—you learned from Noah...

ABBY   Yeah, it's all part of my evil plan. Be quiet.

JULIUS   My baba used to sing me a—Yiddish lullaby.

A pause. Then ABBY *sings, quietly, as a lullaby.*

ABBY   Rothstein the snowman
Was a jolly, happy soul…

JULIUS   Close enough.

ABBY   With an old hash pipe…

JULIUS   I remember this.

(sings quietly) And a Jewish nose…

ABBY   No, I sing. You listen.

(sings quietly) And a brother-in-law named Joel.

JULIUS   Sshhh.

ABBY *stops singing. There's the faint sound of a siren in the distance.*

Hear that? Siren. Somebody else—having—problems too.

ABBY   *(as siren gets louder)* Actually, I think that's for us.

JULIUS   Oh—right—we're famous. *(starts to chuckle again)*

ABBY   Stop that.

JULIUS Sing me.

ABBY Rothstein the snowman
Is meshugeneh, they say,
He's so full of crap—

> *JULIUS appears to have passed out.*

Rothstein? Julius? *Zaydie?*

The siren grows louder.

AUDIENCE SCENE: TEN MORE YEARS

ABBY In the end, I have to confess, I did not save his life.

JULIUS Finally, and then I'll shut up—she saved my life.

ABBY I want to set the record straight about that, because for the next ten years he went on about how I'd saved his life. But the paramedics got there right away, the doctors were great, and they're the ones who did the job.

JULIUS That second heart attack turned out to be a blessing.

ABBY And he came out of the hospital and embarked on one of the most productive decades of his career: renewing his battle to start a Canadian film museum, joining the Canadian Alliance to Legalize Marijuana—whose offices, fittingly, are in his beloved old Loyalist Theatre—and rewriting his screenplay *Scarborough Bluffs*.

JULIUS   Because I'm such an idiot that it took the loss of my dear Phyllis, plus not one but *two* heart attacks, to wake me up from the fantasy that I'd live forever, to the reality that none of us has all the time in the world. Which is why I've been working so hard, and having so much fun at it, these last few years. And it was Abby who's given me these last few years. Plus, of course, whatever future may remain.

ABBY   The work isn't over. We're still hoping to buy the old Winterbottom house to build the museum. And I'm still trying to raise the money to produce *Scarborough Bluffs*. As he always liked to say, *(simultaneously with JULIUS, below)* The downside is, the struggle continues. The upside, however, is that the struggle continues.

JULIUS   The bad news is that the struggle continues. On the other hand, the good news is that the struggle continues.

ABBY   He said so just last month, in the cancer ward, while he was, as usual, arguing about Israel and Palestine with Noah—or, as he always insisted on calling him, Superjew—and cracking up his great-grandkid, Philip, by teaching him gazorps and calling him Rothstein. He also kept thanking me for having given him ten more years. But I said to him, *(to JULIUS)* Rothstein. You've already thanked me. Many times. I mean, come on: you danced at my wedding.

JULIUS   *(continuing toast)* And whenever Noah and I exhaust ourselves with arguing about everything else, we wind up agreeing, one hundred percent, about the only thing that really matters here: that both of us adore our Abby. But now you're all starting to look thirsty. So, in conclusion, a toast to the bride and groom: Noah and Abby. L'chaim!

He toasts, drinks the champagne, and puts down his glass.

So nu, Rothstein-Gideon! Let's dance!

They dance. He is dancing with her at her wedding, while she, at his funeral, is remembering having danced with him when he was alive.

The End

A Glossary Of Jewish Terms, Traditions, and References

Abbeleh: An affectionate diminutive for "Abby."

Aleveh sholem: "May he [she, they] rest in peace."

Alter kacker: "Old guy," "old fart."

Bat mitzvah: A ceremony held to mark the occasion when a girl becomes a woman, under Jewish law, at the age of thirteen.

Bubbie: An affectionate term for grandmother.

Chutzpah: Excessive nerve; gall; egregious boldness.

Daveleh: Like Abbeleh, an affectionate diminutive for "David."

Dreidel: A children's game played during the wintertime Jewish holiday of Hannukah.

Gai gezunterhait: "Go in good health."

Gottenu: A general swear word; "My God."

Hock: To harangue or nag.

Kaddish: The Hebrew prayer spoken by mourners, considered one of the most important and central elements in the Jewish liturgy.

Kvetch: "Complain."

L'chaim: A standard toast, literally meaning "to life."

L'dor v'dor: "From generation unto generation."

Mazel tov: "Congratulations." Literally, "good luck," but in the sense of acknowledging another's good fortune or achievement.

Mensch: A real man, a stand-up guy. Literally, "man."

Meshugeneh: "Crazy."

Mishpocheh: "Family."

Nu: "Well?" "So?" "Next?"

Oy vey's mir: An expression of distress. Literally, "Oh, woe is me."

Reform: A sect of Judaism that seeks to modernize Jewish religious customs and traditions: in Abby's case, the tradition that a person is not considered Jewish or eligible for a bat mitzvah if her mother is not Jewish.

Shabbos: The Jewish Sabbath, which begins at sunset on Friday and ends at sunset on Saturday.

Shiksa: A non-Jewish woman or girl. Often considered derogatory.

Shiva: The period of seven days of mourning after the death of a loved one. Literally, "Seven."

Shmuck: A fool. Literally, a vulgar word for "penis."

Shtup: A vulgarism for sexual intercourse. Sexual intercourse during the Sabbath is highly approved of in the Jewish tradition, though the rabbis would doubtless prefer that the participants be married to each other.

Shul: Synagogue.

Unveiling: In Jewish traditions, the deceased person is buried as soon as possible, but the grave remains unmarked, or marked with only a plain wooden post, for a period after the burial. In some societies the period is a week or thirty days, but in most North American communities it lasts a year. Then the permanent tombstone is unveiled in a graveside ceremony.

Yarmulke: A skullcap worn by Jewish men and boys as a sign of devotion to God.

Zaydie: An affectionate term for grandfather.

Acknowledgements

My thanks to Kim Renders, former artistic director of Theatre Kingston, for committing to have Theatre Kingston produce this play, for guidance in obtaining a grant from Queen's University's Fund for the Support of Artistic Production, and for general encouragement; to Theatre Kingston's subsequent artistic director, Brett Christopher, and actors Sophia Fabiilli and Ian D. Clarke for their participation in the workshop and public reading in November 2011; to members of the audience at that public reading; and to Brett, Sophia, Sam Malkin, Lin Bennett, Katie Bell, and Natasha Nadir, for dramaturgical help.

© Tim Fort

John Lazarus has been an award-winning professional Canadian playwright since 1970. His plays include *Dreaming and Duelling*, *Village of Idiots*, *The Late Blumer*, *The Nightingale*, *David for Queen*, *ICE: beyond cool*, *Rough Magic*, *Trouble on Dibble Street*, *Old Enough to Kill*, and the one-act plays *Babel Rap* and *Medea's Disgust*. Playwrights Canada Press has published his *Homework & Curtains* and his anthology of four short plays for young audiences, *Not So Dumb*. He taught writing for some years at Studio 58, and briefly at the Vancouver Film School and at his alma mater the National Theatre School. He lives with his wife, Lin Bennett, in Kingston, Ontario, where he is a professor in the Drama Department at Queen's University. For more information about John and his writing, please visit www.johnlazarus.ca.

First edition: March 2014
Printed and bound in Canada by Imprimerie Gauvin, Gatineau

Cover design and illustration by Patrick Gray
Book design by Blake Sproule

PLAYWRIGHTS
CANADA PRESS

202-269 Richmond St. W.
Toronto, ON
M5V 1X1

416.703.0013
info@playwrightscanada.com
www.playwrightscanada.com

RECYCLED
Paper made from
recycled material
FSC
www.fsc.org
FSC® C100212